Naples

Footprint

Julius Honnor

Contents

Listings

About the author

Julius Honnor is a writer, editor and photographer living in London but with Italian experiences including teaching English and working on campsites around the Bay of Naples. Born and brought up on the edge of Dartmoor he has travelled the world, taught foreign kids in a Yorkshire village, done a degree in philosophy, designed web pages, worked in bookshops in Plymouth and Kensington, helped build systems for an internet publisher and played lots of football along the way.

Acknowledgements

Thanks to Annarita and family for their kind hospitality and help, to Barbara for tea, Italian conversation and great restaurants, Vincenzo and Marialuisa for parties and Neapolitan tips, to Sarah for corrections and helpdesk advice, but most of all to Clair, for visits, support, enthusiasm and text messages and without whom I couldn't have done any of it.

Naples, stuck between the world's most famous volcano and the deep blue sea, is beautiful and ugly in equal measure. It can be an intimidating place – anarchic and only sporadically law-abiding. The traffic is terrible and peace and quiet is hard to find. But it's an extraordinarily vivacious city, the food (especially pizza) is great, opera, classical music and jazz are ingrained in its culture and the treasure trove of sights hidden away here is at times overwhelming.

Ask an Italian from Rome or the north about Naples and they will throw up their hands in despair and tell you it's a part of Africa. It is indeed dirty, overcrowded and impossibly chaotic – more like Marrakesh than Milan. But probe these gentrified folk a little more, and they may tell you with something approaching admiration about the Neapolitan Renaissance, the cultural rebirth of a once-grand city.

Areas that were considered no-go are now reasonably safe, and *some* of the many churches and monuments semi-permanently closed for "renovation" are now genuinely restored, or at least open, at least some of the time.

Volcanos aside, the city and its surroundings are also geographically blessed: for while the ever-present hulk of Vesuvius bears down on the city, with the fruitful hills of the Sorrento Peninsula plunging to the well-endowed Amalfi Coast on one side and the ornamental beads of Capri, Ischia and Procida out to sea on the other, you're never far away from captivating scenery. Towns and villages cling to cliffs or cluster around harbours in true picture-postcard style and views are colourful and panoramically spectacular. And if it's history you're after, the once-buried wonders of Pompeii and Herculaneum to the east are only slightly more amazing than the ruined marvels of the Campi Flegrei to the west, while to the south, crumbling Paestum is the most majestic of them all.

Naples has a lot of history to get over before it can feel properly at ease with itself. It has a strong but also confused sense of civic pride and tradition: its dialect betrays its mixed parentage, particularly its Spanish and French influences. For hundreds of years it was tossed from one set of rulers to another, and still has a profound anti-establishment feeling, and a distrust of outsiders.

To really understand the psyche of the city, however, it is necessary to look at the relationship between Naples and Vesuvius. Though Neapolitans will feign something like blasé indifference when asked about their volcano, the reality is much more significant. "Il Dominatore", they call Vesuvius, and its glowering presence rising above the city is quite clearly a factor in both the Neapolitans' endemic fatalism and in their hedonistic love of the good life. By extension it can probably be considered partly to blame for Neapolitan driving, extreme levels of superstition and the fact that around signs "severely prohibiting" ball-games, there will almost always be four or five games of football in progress, occasionally using the same signs for goalposts.

At a glance

Santa Lucia

The grandest part of the city centres on the giant and slightly barren piazza del Plebiscito, with its curved colonnade opposite the Palazzo Reale. The vast imposing space, previously a car park, is these days dotted with kids playing football against the backdrop of Vesuvius, glimpsed between grand 17th- and 18th-century buildings. Behind the colonnade the hill of Monte di Dio supports one of Naples' oldest residential areas, its washing hanging out to dry high above the narrow streets. Via Chiaia, running north of the hill, is one of Naples' smartest shopping areas. Also here is the San Carlo opera house and two of Naples' sombre castles: Castel dell'Ovo and Castel Nuovo.

Centro Storico

Though the grandest of Naples' monuments are mainly in Santa Lucia, this area is the heart of the city: its dark, narrow streets greasy, irregularly paved and overflowing with scooters, people and noise. Amongst a plethora of bars and restaurants, small shops sell everything from organic limoncello to electronic water features for nativity scenes. Fascinating churches and *palazzi*, many from the 16th, 17th and 18th centuries, sit beside, or on top of, occasional ancient remnants of 2000 years ago. Sprinkled into the chaos are the city's inconceivably peaceful cloisters. The university is just to the south and the atmosphere here is generally predictably young and loud.

Via Toledo and the Quartieri Spagnoli

Partly pedestrianized via Toledo, Naples' bustling high street, runs between piazza del Plebiscito and piazza Dante. To its west, the narrow streets of the Quartieri Spagnoli are one of the city's poorest areas, and the Camorra heartland. There's a fascinating market every day up via Pignasecca and towards piazza Montesanto, while via Toledo heads north to the Museo Archeologico, with its staggering collection of ancient statues, mosaics and erotica.

Corso Umberto I and around

One of the poorer areas of Central Naples, both economically and in points of interest, this zone is one of Naples' missed opportunities. Though right beside the sea, you can wander the dishevelled streets without ever being aware of its presence. Its highlight is the heaving Mercato di Porta Nolana.

La Sanità and Capodimonte

Beyond the Museo Archeologico the road continues to the fine, green Parco di Capodimonte, where the Palazzo Reale di Capodimonte houses the Bourbon and the Farnese art collections. On a bus there you might not even notice Dickensian La Sanità, lying below, and bypassed by, the bridge built by the French in 1808. With the city's thoroughfare passing above it, the architecture of La Sanità, a dense warren of narrow streets, seems to have been abandoned at the turn of the 19th century. It's fascinating but far from peaceful – despite the fact that it's also where for centuries Naples has buried its dead.

Chiaia, Mergellina and Posillipo

To the west of the centre the genteel Caracciolo seafront curves around to the yacht-filled marina of Mergellina, beyond which the exclusive residential area of Posillipo rises. Chiaia in particular is a more laid-back area of excellent bars, cafés and restaurants, and some pleasant green spaces, notably the Villa Comunale park.

Vomero

This newer, cleaner part of town, up on a hill above the city, is rather like newer, cleaner parts of other Italian cities. For this reason Neapolitans are proud of it, and for the same reason you may be unimpressed. Amid the suburbia, via Scarlatti is a busy shopping street which Neapolitans enjoy wandering up and down, stopping at piazza Vanvitelli for coffee. More exciting are the Castel Sant'Elmo and the Certosa di San Martino, perched high above Naples with, between them, exceptional views and an excellent museum.

★ **Ten of the best**

Best

1 **Cloisters of Santa Chiara, Naples** Orange trees and majolica tiles, p44.

2 **Sant'Anna dei Lombardi, Naples** Magnificent Vasari frescoes, p58.

3 **Porta Nolana market, Naples** Heaving, eclectic and largely illegal, p63.

4 **Museo Archeologico, Naples** Towering Roman statues, fascinating mosaics and ancient porn, p59.

5 **Certosa di San Martino, Naples** Baroque showcase, p73.

6 **Paestum** Enthralling Greek temples, stunning setting, p118.

7 **Cave of the Sibyl, Cuma** Ancient and eerily beautiful, p91.

8 **Monte Solaro, Capri** Vertiginous and spectacularly panoramic, p102.

9 **Marina Corricella, Procida** Colourful and authentically fishy, p107.

10 **Small theatre (Odeon), Pompeii** Perfectly formed and acoustically astonishing, p84.

Around Naples

To the east, Pompeii, Herculaneum and Oplontis are extraordinary museum exhibits preserved by a now-slumbering Vesuvius. Further east the well-groomed Sorrento Peninsula has English tourists aplenty but also a wonderfully fecund landscape. To the west, the volcanic Campi Flegrei still bubble and steam amid more ancient remains. The islands of Capri, Ischia and Procida all have their own style: elegant, beautiful and ragged in turn. To the south, the spectacularly steep and winding Amalfi Coast has beaches and boutiques, while further afield Caserta is an impressive grand old pile and Paestum has more ruins still, in perhaps the most dramatic setting of them all.

Trip planner

Summer in the city can be oppressively hot so it is probably best to do as most Neapolitans do: avoid it. In August the city is semi-deserted and many shops and restaurants are closed. On the other hand, the coast and islands buzz with visitors and festivals at this time. Otherwise, there's not really a bad time to visit. Winter can be rainy, but seldom for long, and, if you're lucky, the wonderfully fresh crisp clear days will give views that stretch for twice as far as those in summer. Concerts, fireworks and the via San Gregorio Armeno crowds make Naples a lively place at Christmas and New Year too. But spring, generally warm and sunny with flower-sprinkled hills, and autumn with its still-warm sea, are the best bets.

Naples in a day
Breakfast on coffee and a sfogliatella at the exceptionally classy *Bar Gambrinus* on piazza Trieste e Trento, followed by a quick stroll around the adjacent piazza del Plebiscito, the grand centre of the city. Don't linger too long though or you'll miss the churches, many of which close at 1230.

Wander up via Toledo to piazza Carità, where you can head right to piazza Monteoliveto, where Sant'Anna dei Lombardi has a stunning collection of Renaissance frescoes and sculpture. Just along from here is piazza del Gesù, and the beginning of the atmospheric Centro Storico, the heart of old Naples. A good circuit from here would be to stroll down 'Spaccanapoli', the long straight road which heads east from here to via Duomo, and take a look at the Duomo (cathedral) itself before heading back along via Tribunali. Along the way there are plenty of churches you can take in, but don't miss the beautiful cloisters of Santa Chiara or the Caravaggio altarpiece in Pio Monte della Misericordia.

For **lunch** try the excellent *Cantina di via Sapienza*, just to the north, or head west into the Quartieri Spagnoli for a real taste of Neapolitan home cooking at *Trattoria Casillo Enzo*.

★ Five of the best views

1 Castel Sant'Elmo/Certosa di San Martino Those monks must have spent a large proportion of their time looking out over the city. The steps from here to the Centro Storico have good views around almost every bend.

2 Monte Echia Part of a long-extinct volcano crater (another part is the island on which Castel dell'Ovo now stands), this is a pretty good view without having to go up anything too exerting, and is only a short walk from piazza del Plebiscito.

3 Vesuvius Most go up Vesuvius to see the crater, and to feel a sense of the power of the thing. It's also worth going up, however, just so you can look down.

4 Monte Solaro, Capri With views almost straight down to the sea 589m below, as well as all around to the Sorrento Peninsula and beyond, this takes some beating. It's quite a climb but there is a chairlift if you're feeling lazy.

5 Castello Aragonese, Ischia In just about every direction you look from this ancient stronghold there are amazing views, be they of distant Capri across the sea, of the mountains of the mainland or (best of all) of Ischia itself.

In the **afternoon** head further north up via Toledo and its continuations to the extraordinary Museo Archeologico, filled with Roman sculptures and mosaics. Don't miss out either on the intriguing *Gabinetto Segreto*, a room of ancient pornography. By the time you've finished here the shops should be open again after their siesta and you can wander back down via Toledo, stopping en route at *Gelateria Scimmia* (piazza Carità) for an excellent ice-cream.

From your starting point on piazza Trieste e Trento the smart shopping street of via Chiaia heads west to Chiaia itself. Along here too is *Brandi*, Naples' most famous pizzeria (should you be hungry again). Alternatively continue into Chiaia and find one of its excellent **restaurants**. *La Cantina di Albi Cocca* is a good option if you want to stay out late as it has excellent food alongside a long wine and beer list.

If you're still up for more, Chiaia is also one of the best areas for **clubs**: try *Velvet* or *Tongue* on via dei Mille, both of which will keep you busy until well into the early hours.

A weekend

You could spend day one in the city, exploring the Centro Storico, visiting the Museo Archeologico, doing some shopping, drinking coffee and eating pizza and ice-cream.

The second day could then be used for an excursion, either to one of the islands or maybe to Pompeii and Vesuvius, or south to the extraordinary ancient Greek remains at Paestum.

A third day would give you the opportunity to see more of the city's sights, perhaps the spectacular **Certosa di San Martino** (an old monastery) on top of the hill above the city, the **Palazzo Reale** or the excellent art collection at **Capodimonte**, followed by an exploration of the lovely area of **Chiaia**, and west to the marina of **Mergellina**, with its great views of the city as the sun sets.

A week

A week in and around the city gives you time to explore the Centro Storico properly as well as take in more of the city's many good museums, castles and palaces. It's also long enough to see more of the history outside the city, such as **Herculaneum**, **Oplontis** or **Cuma** and the **Campi Flegrei**. The **Amalfi Coast** is also reachable, and you might want to stay over, perhaps in **Ravello**, which makes an excellent base for walks and for exploring the area, and where you could also go to a classical music concert. Alternatively you might want to spend a couple of days on one of the islands. **Capri** is the more standard choice, though **Ischia** is equally beautiful and **Procida** is more unspoilt.

Contemporary Naples

Pouring scorn on the so-called Neapolitan Renaissance, some Neapolitans consider that excessive money has been spent on the city's 'beautiful areas', and not enough on the rest, some of which is very obviously crying out for investment. While on the surrounding islands, and on the Amalfi Coast, life continues to be distinctly privileged, it is undeniably the case that in Naples within a few hundred metres of its grand historic monuments, families live in squalor, in tiny houses or *bassi*, often comprising only a single room.

The truth is probably that although some of the mentality of the city has changed in the last 10 years, it will take much more investment over a long period before the city starts to draw the numbers of tourists its attractions justify. This is a vicious circle, since the tourists are really needed now in order to generate the money for further renovation and development. The city of Naples currently has a hole in its finances and it's hard to see how this will be filled. Beggars are a common sight and unemployment remains high, very high among women and the young (it peaks for young women at above 60%). The consensus about solutions that the once much-vaunted Antonio Bassolino created after he became Naples' mayor in 1993 has now broken down slightly. The early Bassolino years were marked by a wave of optimism and civic pride in the city and an extraordinary turnaround in Naples' image in the rest of the country. Bassolino has now become the regional governor and has been succeeded by Rosa Russo Iervolino and although the political make-up of the administration has changed little, there is less agreement about the way forward.

This ambivalence to 'progress' was also apparent when, in January 2002, Naples was dragged into the Eurozone with scant enthusiasm but more of a shrug than a protest. There was little love for the lira, but old habits die hard and in many shops prices are still added up in the old currency before being converted.

Things are still changing slowly, however. The newly renovated, and partly pedestrianized piazza Dante, complete with a new metro station, is a good example of the knock-on advantages urban renewal can bring. Neapolitans hope that when the rest of the new metro extension comes on line, other parts of the city will benefit similarly. Occasional traffic-free mornings in the city centre show how different it could be if it wasn't constantly clogged with honking, polluting traffic but it will take more than a new metro line to seriously loosen the car's current stranglehold.

The city's other enormous problem is its lawlessness: although Naples' reputation for being a dangerous city is massively exaggerated, petty crime, largely bag-snatching, pick-pocketing and car-theft, are still rife. More seriously, though largely out of sight of the average tourist, organized crime still controls a sizeable proportion of the city, from fruit and vegetables and car parking 'attendants' to drug dealing and counterfeit goods. Furthermore, gangland killings between different Camorra factions continue, and the attitudes the Camorra have engendered in more than 50 years of de facto power are deeply ingrained into the structure and psyche of the city. Corruption and a lack of respect for the law are endemic and continue, largely unquestioned, to be an integral part of the Neapolitan way of life. The president of Napoli football club was recently arrested for his supposed involvement in a scam where fake paintings were being sold through a local television shopping channel. Prior to that, the Cardinal of Naples was the subject of an inquiry into allegations of loan sharking. This sort of story surprises nobody in Naples.

More a focus of attention in the first years of the 21st century has been Naples' strong 'No Global' movement, and especially the events that surrounded the riots of March 2001 at the Global Forum meeting in the city. Eighty activists were allegedly dragged out of hospital, sodomized, tortured, and forced to kiss photos of Mussolini by police in the Raniero barracks. In April 2002 eight police officers were arrested for their part in the affair, and

Vesuvius from Santa Lucia
Even in the centre of the city Vesuvius is a presence and an icon, glimpsed between buildings, sitting on the horizon or imagined through smog.

investigations continue into another 100. The entire process has become highly politically charged, with the right-wing national government attacking prosecutors for being politically biased.

Whether it is in the arena of organized crime or anti-globalization, contemporary Naples still tends to steer it own course, mostly against the grain. On the surface the city's religiosity is a much more conventional and conservative element. However, although Catholicism continues to be a vital component of Neapolitan life, here it is a religion which has as much in common with African Christianity as with the more orthodox version which emanates from the Vatican just 200 miles away. Superstition is rife and morbid traditions from ancient cults, such as praying to the skulls of the deceased, continue to exert a strong hold over much of the population. The miracles of San Gennaro (see p51) are vital to psychological well-being for many.

The city's old Baroque and operatic traditions also continue to be strongly felt culturally though in this respect the city is slowly entering the 21st century: Bassolino's initiatives to have contemporary art installations every Christmas in piazza del Plebiscito continue to attract attention and various new developments will increase the space for contemporary art. Musically, the city continues to produce bands that use local dialect to create a distinctive Neapolitan sound and this Neapolitan musical scene also stretches to jazz and rap, though there is a trend towards the Italian mainstream among those who become successful. Mostly, however, the cultural focus remains on the golden eras of the past, and here there are some struggles: the San Carlo opera house may be the second most prestigious in the country, arguably in the world, but financially it seems barely to keep its head above water.

The big Neapolitan question is not 'how much has the city changed?' but 'how deep do the changes go?' Underneath some beautification and despite a new-found sense of self-confidence, some serious and fundamental problems still need addressing.

From the UK, Naples presents no problem in terms of its accessibility. The quickest and cheapest way of getting to the city is to take advantage of the no-frills airlines, either to Naples itself or to reasonably-nearby Rome. It is, of course, possible to take the train all the way from London (via Paris and Rome) but, despite being an infinitely more civilized way of travelling, this will take the best part of a day and cost considerably more. If you intend to drive, allow at least two days. From North America you will need to fly to Rome or Milan and change there. There are no direct flights to Italy from Australasia, and a stopover in London is probably your best bet.

Public transport has improved massively in the last few years in Naples and is now good and generally reliable. Buses cover most of the city and the surrounding area and there is also a relatively comprehensive rail network, including a metro system in the city and, of course, the good old funiculars of *Funiculì Funiculà* fame.

Getting there

Air

From the UK and the rest of Europe *Go* fly twice daily from London Stansted to Naples. Book ahead and prepare to be flexible and you may get a return for as little as £50. Occasional special offers may be even better than this. At short notice, and at weekends and holiday periods, these prices can rise to £150 or more.

Alternatively, if you are prepared to take a more roundabout journey, it might be worth checking *Ryanair* for cheap flights to Rome, and doing the rest by train. *Ryanair* buses connect the airport with Rome Termini train station, from where there are frequent (approximately twice hourly) trains to Naples (a two-hour journey).

British Airways (Naples airport office **T** 081-7803087) run three services a day to London Gatwick. *Transavia* fly daily to and from Amsterdam. *Alitalia* fly to other Italian cities and to Paris. *Air France* also have daily flights to and from Paris.

From North America There are no direct flights to Naples from the US or Canada. Rome is the nearest place you can fly to, but most direct flights from the US go to Milan. *Alitalia* fly direct to Rome (and Milan) from New York and Toronto, as do *Delta Airlines*, but otherwise you will have to stop over (in a European city) before connecting to Naples. Flights start from around US$500 in low season, and from Los Angeles (usually via New York) will be nearer US$650 (in high season this can rise to over US$1,500). Other airlines that fly to Naples from the US via other European cities include: *Air France, American Airlines, British Airways, Iberia, KLM, Lufthansa*.

From Australia and New Zealand There are no direct flights to Naples (or anywhere else in Italy) from either Australia or New Zealand. You will have to change at least twice. You can fly to Milan and Rome via another European or Asian (eg Singapore, Kuala Lumpur) city, from where you will have to connnect again for Naples.

Airlines that fly to European cities from Australia and New Zealand include: *Alitalia, British Airways, Lufthansa, Malaysian Airlines, Qantas, Singapore Airlines, Virgin Atlantic*. The cost low season is likely to be at least A$1,700, rising to A$2,500 during high season.

Airport information **Naples airport (Capodichino)** is small enough to be easily manageable. It's also not far from the city

 Airlines and agents

Airlines

Alitalia, **T** 0874-5448259, www.alitalia.it
Air France, **T** 0845-0845 111, www.airfrance.com
British Airways **T** 0845-7733377, www.britishairways.com
Delta, **T** 1800-2414141, www.delta.com
Go, **T** 0870-6076543, www.gofly.com
KLM, **T** 0870-5074047, www.klm.com
Lufthansa, **T** 0845-7737747, www.lufthansa.com
Malaysia Air, **T** 618-453-2113, www.malaysiaair.com
Qantas, **T** 0845-7747767, www.qantas.com
Ryanair, **T** 0871-2460000, www.ryanair.com
Singapore Airlines, **T** 213-1011, www.singaporeair.com
Transavia Airlines, **T** 20-4060400, www.transavia.nl
Virgin Atlantic, **T** 1800-8628621, www.virgin-atlantic.com

Agents
www.cheapflights.com
www.expedia.com
www.flynow.com
www.istc.org
www.statravel.com
www.travelocity.com

centre, making onward travel fairly easy. Buses to the centre (see below) are fairly good and you can connect to other services here. The information desk between the check-in area and the arrivals area is helpful (you can pick up a free copy of *Qui Napoli* here, see p31, check the latest tourist information and get some useful timetables). Flight info: **T** 848-888777 or **T** 081-7896259, www.gesac.it, 0530-0030. There are also a few shops and cafés.

There's a hotel reservation desk (*Promotel*, 0900-2330) at the end of the airport near arrivals, a cashpoint which accepts cirrus and credit cards, and a *cambio* (bureau de change) as well as a couple of cafés and gift shops. For car hire details see p25.

Airport buses   The **3S Bus** ('Service, Save money and Satisfaction') runs every 15 minutes from 0600 until 2330 from outside the terminal building to the port via the Central Station in piazza Garibaldi (see below). Journey times are approximately 15 minutes to piazza Garibaldi and half an hour to the port. Despite its name, it's actually a standard ANM orange city bus. Tickets are available from the hotel reservation desk, or from tabacchi or newsstands, for €0.77. It arrives and departs from outside Departures.

The swish, privately run **CLP** airport bus stopped running in spring 2002 but there should be a replacement service, probably running direct between the airport and the port of Naples. Ask at the Promotel desk for details. Take this bus to get to the **islands**. There are also six services a day to **Sorrento** run by *Curreri* (€5.20, 1 hour, **T** 081-8015420). Again, tickets are available from the hotel reservation desk in the airport.

Taxis   A taxi to the centre of Naples shouldn't cost more than €20, no more than €15 to piazza Garibaldi.

Rail
National and international train services stop at Naples on the Sicily-Milan route. Book or find details through *Rail Europe*

T 0870-5848848 (from UK), www.raileurope.co.uk. General train information in Italy: **T** 848-888088, www.trenitalia.com, 0700-2100. A combination of a return on the **Paris-Rome** night train and a 3-day all-Italy 'Domino' pass costs about £150, cheaper than an ordinary ticket all the way. London-Paris on Eurostar is around £80 return. *Club Eurostar*, in Italy (**T** 081-286996, www.trenitalia.com – and no relation to the London-Paris link) has information and timetables in English and allows you to buy some tickets online.

Train station At the eastern end of piazza Garibaldi, frequent mainline trains arrive at **Napoli Centrale** from Rome and from the south. Longer-distance trains also come from Milan, Bologna and Florence. Eurostar services arrive at a part of the station which is confusingly called **Napoli Piazza Garibaldi**, even though it's part of the same complex. Mainline trains are useful for trips to Paestum and Caserta, see p26. Tickets must be stamped with the date in a validating machine on the platform before use.

Metro trains (see p26) on Linea 2 also leave from here to Montesanto, Chiaia (piazza Amadeo), Mergellina, Campi Flegrei and Pozzuoli. The Circumvesuviana (see p26) is underneath the Stazione Centrale, a level down.

Bus
Though there is no centralized **bus station**, most long-distance buses arrive and leave from various locations around piazza Garibaldi. *CTP* (**T** 081-7001111) and *STP* (**T** 081-5522176) are two of the biggest companies. There is an information desk in the middle of the piazza (see p28 for ticket information). Piazza Garibaldi is anarchic, traffic-clogged and not a very pleasant place but it's hard to avoid. It's worth trying to work out the next stage of your journey before you get there. The 3S airport bus arrives at the western end of the piazza, near the statue of Garibaldi himself, handy for the R2 bus (see below). It departs from the other end, to the left of the Stazione Centrale, just outside McDonald's.

Getting around

Bus

Some of the most useful buses are frequent and efficient. These are prefixed with an 'R' and generally come at least every 10 minutes. If you want to go anywhere outside the centre, however, you may have to wait a while longer. **R2** buses do the route from piazza Garibaldi along corso Umberto I to piazza Trieste e Trento. **R3** buses run from piazza Carità to Mergellina via piazza Trieste e Trento and the Chiaia seafront. **www.anm.it** has decent timetables, details of bus services in the city, and an excellent big map.

There are five buses a day from Naples to **Amalfi** (leaving from the *SITA* station, **T** 081-5522176, 200 m east of the Molo Beverello port, €3.15, 1 hr 55 mins), the first at 1000, the last returning at 1830. Bus **152** runs from piazza Garibaldi in Naples to **Pozzuoli**, **Baia** (for **Cuma**) and beyond, stopping at **Solfatara** and the amphitheatre. *SITA* buses from Naples to **Salerno** also stop at **Pompeii**.

Ravello is only reachable by taking the local bus up the hill from Amalfi. **Positano** is best reached by bus from Sorrento. There are *CTP* buses every 20 minutes from piazza Garibaldi to **Caserta**, 1 hr, **T** 081-7001111. **Paestum** is reachable by bus only by changing in Salerno.

Car hire

Driving in or around Naples can't be recommended. In the city itself traffic is hellish, and rules of the road are all but meaningless. Parking is difficult at the best of times and when you find a space you'll invariably be faced with a camorra-run protection racket where you'll be asked for money by someone offering to 'look after' your car. There is the added hassle of the possibility of car-theft. The Amalfi Coast road is best left to those who've done it before and there is no real reason to take a car onto the islands.

Avis, Aeroporto di Capodichino **T** 081-7805790; piazza Garibaldi **T** 081-5543020. *Hertz*, Aeroporto di Capodichino **T** 081-7802971;

piazza Garibaldi **T** 081-206228. *Maggiore*, Aeroporto di
Capodichino **T** 081-5521900; piazza Garibaldi **T** 081-287858. **NB**
Renting cars is usually cheaper if arranged from home.

Rail
Metro Naples' metro system is being extended, and **Linea 1** will
eventually cover useful central areas such as corso Umberto I.
Currently, you're unlikely to want to use this line much, although it
does connect piazza Dante and the Museo Archeologico to piazza
Vanvitelli every half hour. You may find **Linea 2** useful for
connecting piazza Garibaldi (central station) to Montesanto, Chiaia
(piazza Amadeo), Mergellina, Campi Flegrei (Pozzuoli-Solfatara),
Bagnoli and Stadio San Paolo. **T** 800-568866.

Circumvesuviana This useful train line runs from Naples' piazza
Garibaldi around the Bay to Sorrento every half an hour or so, stopping at Torre Annunziata (for **Oplontis**), **Pompeii** ('Pompeii
Scavi') and **Herculaneum** ('Ercolano') along the way,
T 081-7722444. If you're going both ways it's worth buying a daily
(*giornaliero*) Unico ticket, Fascia 5 for €5.16, which also lets you
use local buses (though not those of *SITA*) at no extra cost.

Local trains **Ferrovia Cumana** (**T** 800-00166) trains leave
Montesanto station in the Quartieri Spagnoli on the route along
the coast to **Pozzuoli**, **Baia** and **Cuma**. They run every 10
minutes during the day, every 20 minutes in the evening, until
2120. There is also a **Ferrovia Circumflegrea** line from
Montesanto which does an inland version of the same route. It
doesn't go anywhere you'd specially want to go though. There is a
stop called Cuma on this line but it's a long way from the ruins.

Mainline trains Trains (those for **Paola**) go direct from Naples'
Stazione Centrale to **Paestum** four or five times a day, taking an
hour and a half and costing €9.50 return. To **Caserta**, trains run

several times an hour, journey time 40 mins. Caserta is in Unico zone 4, for which a day ticket costs €4.96. www.trenitalia.com has easy-to-use timetables for mainline trains in English.

Funicular Naples' funiculars, celebrated in the classic Neapolitan song *Funiculì Funiculà*, all go up the hill to Vomero from various parts of the city. There are four funiculars, **Centrale** (via Toledo to piazza Fuga), **Chiaia** (via del Parco Margherita to via Cimarosa), **Montesanto** (piazza Montesanto to via Morghen) and **Mergellina** (via Mergellina to via Manzoni). For some reason the standard 90-minute tickets only allow one funicular journey. **T** 800-568866.

Sea

There is a comprehensive network of ferry and hydrofoil routes leaving from the main port of Molo Beverello, near Castel Nuovo, to the islands and to Sorrento, and, in summer, to the Amalfi Coast. Some hydrofoils also depart from the Mergellina quay. *Qui Napoli* has timetables though *Il Mattino* has a more complete and up-to-date list. Tickets are available from all companies at the port.

You can catch a hydrofoil from Naples to the Marina Piccola in **Sorrento**. There are also hydrofoil and ferry services between Sorrento and Capri, and a hydrofoil service to Ischia from April to October (see below).

There are frequent ferry and hydrofoil services between Naples and **Ischia**, **Procida** and **Capri**. Ferries are run by *Caremar* (**T** 081-5513882) and *Linee Lauro* (**T** 081-5522838, www.lineelauro.it), hydrofoils by *Caremar*, *SNAV* (**T** 081-7612348), *NLG* (Capri only, **T** 081-5527209) and *Alilauro* (**T** 081-5522838).

Linee Lauro also operate ferries from **Pozzuoli** to **Ischia** via **Procida**. *Caremar*, *Alilauro* and *NLG* go from **Sorrento** to **Capri**. *Alilauro* also go from **Sorrento** to **Ischia**. There are also summer services to **Capri** from **Amalfi** via **Positano** run by *Alicost* (**T** 089-227979).

The ferry journey from Naples takes about an hour to Procida, an hour and a half to Ischia and an hour and 20 minutes to Capri. Hydrofoils take about half the time.

Prices vary slightly from company to company but a return on the ferry to Ischia or Capri costs about €10, to Procida about €8. Hydrofoils cost about twice as much.

Ferries arrive and depart from the main Molo Beverello port two or three times daily to and from **Palermo** (*Tirrenia*, **T** 199-123199; *SNAV*, **T** 081-7612348) and two or three times a week to the **Aeolian Islands** (*Siremar*, **T** 081-5800340). There are less frequent services to Cagliari in **Sardinia** (weekly, *Tirrenia*, **T** 199-123199/ 081-7201111), and to **Tunis** (weekly, *Linee Lauro*, **T** 081-5513352).

Walking

For most of the city, certainly the old part, the best way to get around is to walk. The biggest problem with this strategy is the traffic. Cars and scooters rattle down roads barely wide enough to walk down, and expect you to get out of their way. The only solution is to do as the Neapolitans do: take your time and don't be hurried by the constant honking. Despite first impressions the odds are that they won't run you over. But crossing roads in Naples is an art form – in many cases the only way you'll get across is to find half a gap, grab the opportunity, and push through, confidently stopping the traffic. This may not save your life, but it may be the only way to get to the other side.

Tickets

Naples has a single (though not entirely simple) ticket system for all its public transport. Tickets must be purchased before boarding buses or trains, and must be validated. You can get them at any tabacchi (these all display a large 'T' sign outside), stations and at many newsstands. It's worth buying a few tickets and saving them until you need them.

Tickets must be validated when you get on buses: place the end with the arrow into the stamping machine (there are usually two on each bus at the front and back). Your ticket will be printed with the date and time, and is valid on buses, trams, funiculars and the metro for 90 minutes or more from this time (though, confusingly, only for one funicular journey). When you use your ticket to go through a barrier, as on the metro, it will be stamped for you.

There are two types of tickets: **GiraNapoli** covers the city and **Unico** goes further afield. If you simply ask for '*un biglietto*' (or '*due biglietti*' etc) you will get a GiraNapoli ticket. These tickets cost €0.77 each but it's also possible to buy a day-ticket for €2.32. Unico tickets come in different flavours: Zone 1 to Zone 5, covering progressively wider areas. They cost between €1.29 and €2.84, and are valid for 100 (zone 1) up to 180 minutes (zone 5). Unico tickets cover almost all forms of public transport in Naples and the surrounding areas, and can be useful for trips to Pompeii or Sorrento for example (Unico Fascia 1 tickets cover Pozzuoli, Fascia 2 also covers Cuma and Baia). Day versions of these are also available ('*un biglietto giornaliero*'), and are usually what you will get if you ask for a return ('*andante e ritorno*') since they cost double the single price.

Tours and tourist information

Tours

Many tours (most of them free) take place during **Maggio dei Monumenti** (see Festivals, p189). Often these are of buildings closed to the public for the rest of the year.

Interesting, and slightly alternative, often historically themed tours around and outside the city (usually every Sunday) are organized by **Legambiente**, an ecological group working to improve the life of the city. Vico della Quercia 7, **T/F** 081-4203161 neapolis@hotmail.com   See www.napolisworld.it for the forthcoming programme.

More conventional tours are run by various agencies: **Project Napoli Service**, via Orazio 31, **T** 081-5586107; tour of the city's

napoli>artecard

Introduced in spring 2002 to an enormous and somewhat disproportionate amount of hype, the napoli>artecard is a card which for 60 hours gives you free entry into two museums and half-price entrance into four more as well as free travel in the city and some other discounts such as 20% off ferry and hydrofoil tickets. It costs €13, or €8 if you're under 25, and is probably a worthwhile investment if you plan to visit more than one museum. It's valid for the city's six big museums: the Museo Archeologico, the Museo di Capodimonte, the Certosa e Museo di San Martino, the Museo Civico di Castel Nuovo, the Castel Sant'Elmo and the Palazzo Reale. There is also a rather infrequent weekend bus service for exclusive use of artecard holders, which runs between all the attractions.
www.napoliartecard.com, **T** 800-600601/063-9967650

 Italian State Tourist Board (ENIT) offices abroad

UK 1 Princes St, London W1R 8AY **T** 020-74081254,
F 020-74936695 enitlondon@globalnet.co.uk
USA 630 Fifth Avenue, Suite 1565, New York NY 10111,
T 212-2454822, **F** 212-5869249 www.italiantourism.com;
12400 Wilshire Blvd, Suite 550, Los Angeles, CA 90025,
T 310-8200098, **F** 310-8206357; 500 North Michigan Av, Suite 2240, Chicago IL 60611, **T** 312-6440996, **F** 0312-6443019
enitch@italiantourism.com
Canada 1 Place Ville-Marie, Suite 1914, Montreal QC H3B 2C3,
T 0514-8667667, **F** 0514-3921429
Australia Level 26, 44 Market St, Sydney, NSW 2000,
T 02-92621666, **F** 02-92621677 enitour@ihug.com.au

sights. **Meta Felix Tour**, via Partenope 12, **T** 081-7645808; panoramic tour of Naples and Solfatara, walking tour of the Centro Storico, and other tours out of the city. **Della Penna Tour**, via Argine 506, **T** 081-5614233; Naples by night as well as tours to the Campi Flegrei and the Amalfi Coast.

There are also two fascinating tours of the ancient aqueducts underneath Naples, run by **Napoli Sotterranea**, see p41 and p55.

Tourist information

Naples   Tourist information offices around Naples are confusingly (though somewhat typically) run by three different organizations. They all tend to have more or less the same material, however. The most useful and helpful is probably the office of the **Azienda autonoma di soggiorno, cura e turismo** in the Centro Storico, piazza del Gesù, **T** 081-5523328. *Mon-Sat 0900-2000, Sun 0900-1500.* Another well-placed office is under the colonnade in piazza del Plebiscito (**Osservatorio turistico-culturale del Comune**, Portico di San Francesco di Paola, piazza Plebiscito, **T** 081-2471123). Other offices can be found at the airport (see above), at the central station, at Mergellina station, opposite the San Carlo opera house and in piazza dei Martiri.

Make sure to pick up the useful bi-lingual monthly publication *Qui Napoli*, which is free and full of the most up-to-date information, timetables and events. Alternatively you can download it in pdf format before you go from the the official tourist board site for Naples, www.inaples.it. Other useful websites include: **www.napoli.com** (up-to-date information on news and events in the city); **www.italydaily.it** (excellent daily Italian news service in English); **www.napolinapoli.com** (very thorough and particularly good on events and culture in the city but until the long-promised English version is finished it is only in Italian).

Amalfi   corso delle Repubbliche Marinare 27, **T** 089-871107.

Campi Flegrei The helpful tourist office in Pozzuoli will very happily provide you with a monthly brochure *Welcome to the Phlegrean Fields*, which has maps of Pozzuoli and the surrounding area. Piazza Matteotti 1/a, **T** 081-5266639, **F** 081-5265068, www.giubileo.regione.campania.it, www.campnet.it/aziendaturismo/pozzuoli *Mon-Fri 0900-1400, 1500-1540.*

The islands Capri, piazza Umberto I, **T** 081-8370686; Ischia, corso Vittoria Colonna 116, **T** 081-5074211; Positano: via del Saracino 4, **T** 089-875067.

Sorrento Peninsula Inside the Foreigners' Club, just beyond piazza San Antonio, to the north of piazza Tasso, via Luigi de Maio 35, **T** 081-8074033, **F** 081-8773397, www.sorrentotourism.it They will provide you with a good map of the town as well as photocopied Circumvesuviana train timetables and walking maps.

Paestum There's an office north of the museum, which can give you an illustrated booklet including a simple map of the site. *Azienda Autonoma Soggiorno e Turismo*, via Magna Grecia 887/891, **T** 082-8811016, **F** 082-8722322, www.comune.capaccio.sa.it *0900-1300, also 1400-1700 during busy periods.* A handful of small shops and cafés line the road beside the site selling postcards, guidebooks and fairly dire sandwiches.

Pompeii The Pompeii tourist office also covers the area's other sites: Herculaneum, Oplontis and Stabia. Good Pompeii site maps are available free from the office at the main Porta Marina entrance. You can also rent audio guides. **T** 081-8575347, www.pompeiisites.org

Ravello piazza Duomo, **T** 089-857096, www.ravello.it/azienda turismoaziendaturismo@ravello.it Will supply you with maps of walking paths and other information.

Naples

Santa Lucia 35 Naples' centre, if not quite its heart. Castles and cafés, an enormous piazza, strolling grown-ups and football-playing kids.

Centro Storico 43 Dark and greasy, Roman Spaccanapoli and via dei Tribunali are still the backbones of the city. Students, street sellers, scooters and cloisters.

Via Toledo and the Quartieri Spagnoli 57
A contemporary pedestrianized street holds back the old labyrinth of the Camorra heartland. Buskers, restaurants, ancient artefacts and organized crime.

Corso Umberto I and around 62 A transport hub and thoroughfare, a university on one side, a market on the other. Museums, fish and contraband.

La Sanità and Capodimonte 64 A green hill and a grey valley. A park, an art gallery and Paleo-Christian catacombs.

Chiaia, Mergellina and Posillipo 69
Smart seafront Naples. Yachts, designer shops, disco-dancing and dirty beaches.

Vomero 73 A cooler Neapolitan suburb up on the hill. A castle, a monastery and amazing views.

Santa Lucia: the grand centre

*Piazza del Plebiscito forms the grand centrepiece of the city. It's flanked on its east side by the **Palazzo Reale** (Royal Palace) and by a semi-circular colonnade and the church of **San Francesco di Paola** on the other. Behind the church on the hill of Monte di Dio, tightly packed housing is stacked on the area where the original Parthenope was founded in around 680BC by Greeks from nearby Cuma.*

*The grandiose theme is continued throughout the rest of this area: the **Teatro di San Carlo**, Naples' great opera house, is on the busy adjoining piazza Trieste e Trento, as are some of the city's best cafés. The city's two castles are also here, the honey-coloured **Castel dell'Ovo** to the south, and the towering **Castel Nuovo** (better known as the Maschio Angioino) behind the port to the east.*

▸▸ *See Sleeping p125, Arts and entertainment p177, Shopping p193*

 ## Sights

Piazza del Plebiscito
Chiesa San Francesco di Paola: *Mon-Fri 0800-1200, 1530-1800; Sat and Sun 0800-1300. Map 3, F4, p250*

A chaotic microcosm of Naples' traffic problems until 1994, when it was pedestrianized, if not quite the heart of the city, the piazza has at least become a good place to wander in one's finest clothes on a Sunday afternoon. It's also used for concerts, events and demonstrations and is as good a location as any to start a Neapolitan holiday.

The neoclassical **Colonnade** (1809) with its Doric columns dominates the piazza and predates the **Chiesa di San Francesco di Paola** in its centre, which was added in 1817. It's a good, though dirty, place to sit and watch the world go by. The church, modelled on the Pantheon in Rome, is not held in great esteem by Neapolitans, perhaps because of its ostentatious Roman

> ### Nightlights
>
> Every evening, at sunset, the colonnade and church of San Francesco di Paola in piazza del Plebiscito are lit up, with the help of triumphal piped classical music, and turned into something reminiscent of a scene from *Star Wars*.
>
> In theory at least, the lights change colour, from yellow on the hour, to a rather shocking shade of pink at a quarter past, to green at half past and to a vivid blue at a quarter to. The reality, however, seems to be something a little more randomly chaotic, in typically Neapolitan style.

derivation, and seems a little under-used, despite its prestigious position and an impressive domed interior.

The **statues** along the front of the Royal Palace are various past rulers of the city. Added in 1888 they are, chronologically and from left to right, Roger II, Emperor Frederick II, Charles of Anjou, Alfonso of Aragon, Emperor Charles V, Charles III of Bourbon, Joachim Murat and Victor Emmanuel II.

The two statues on horseback (by Antonio Canova) in the centre of the piazza are Charles III of Bourbon (on the left) and his son and successor Ferdinando, who built the church behind him.

Monte Echia
Map 3, I3, p251

To orientate yourself and to get a great view of the city (indeed the whole bay on a clear day), head up the hill to the right of the colonnade and turn left along via Egiziaca a Pizzofalcone to reach the top of the ex-volcano Monte Echia, dominated to the west by the

! The film *Ieri, Oggi, Domani*, starring Sophia Loren, was filmed on via Egiziaca a Pizzofalcone and the Rampa di Pizzofalcone.

★ Piazzas Trieste e Trento and del Plebiscito
Piazza del Plebiscito is an unusually quiet space. Piazza Trieste e Trento, on the other hand, has the traditional Neapolitan elements of traffic, people, gesticulating traffic police and great coffee.

Nunziatella military academy. At the summit of the hill there are some rather indistinct remains of the original Greek city.

To see another side of Naples from the grandiosity of the piazza del Plebiscito, continue south down the **Rampa di Pizzofalcone**, a zig-zagging set of steps which pass tiny houses chiselled out of the mountain, before coming out on Chiatamone near Castel dell'Ovo. A short walk to the left will take you back into the heart of Santa Lucia.

L'Archivio Fotografico Parisio
piazza del Plebiscito/largo Carolina, **T** 081-7645122. *Mon-Sun 0930-1330 but to 1800 from largo Carolina. Free.* Map 3, F3, p250

The Parisio Photographic Archive is the only good use of space in the piazza del Plebiscito colonnade. A small but interesting collection of photographs of Naples past is exhibited around the walls and there is a decent collection of photographic books for sale.

Palazzo Reale
T 081-7944021. *Daily except Wed, 0900-2000. Ticket office closes at 1900. Entrance to Royal Apartments €4, courtyard and gardens of the palace are free. The ticket office is well-hidden at the far end of the bookshop near to the piazza del Plebiscito entrance, which is often closed (in which case enter from piazza Trieste e Trento). Information on each room is posted in Italian and English.* Map 3, F5, p250

The Royal Palace, opposite the colonnade on piazza del Plebiscito, includes gardens, the grand but fusty national library (see p220), and the Royal Apartments, used by the Spanish and Austrian viceroys and the Bourbon kings and queens. Designed by Neapolitan architect Domenico Fontana the palace was built at the beginning of the 17th century for the Spanish viceroys and extended by the Bourbons in the 18th century.

It's easy to imagine royalty making their way up the suitably grand **Scalone Monumentale** (Grand Staircase, renovated after a fire in 1837), which you climb in order to reach the **Royal Apartments**. Once there, highlights include the ornate Court Theatre, dramatic ceiling frescoes by Belisario Corenzio (c1622) in both the Second Anteroom and the Ambassadors' Hall, and also those of Giovanni Battista Caracciolo in the Sala del Gran Capitano. One in the latter is a picture of Caravaggio.

In the Throne Room, a proper fairytale throne, complete with lions on the arms and an eagle at the back, is almost too tempting not to sit on. The golden female figures on the ceiling represent the 14 districts of the Sicilian Kingdom in the early 19th century.

Foremost among an impressive collection of clocks is an elaborate piece of engineering in the Flemish Hall made in London by Charles Clay in 1730 which doubles as a music box.

What appears to be a waterwheel in room XXIII is actually a rotating desk which allowed Queen Maria Carolina to look at several books at the same time without moving from her seat.

Leave some energy for the **Cappella Reale** (Palatine Chapel), even grander than the rest of the palace. Pride of place here is given not to the sparkling altar or the bright frescoes but *il Presepe del Banco di Napoli* (The Nativity of the Bank of Napoli), an extreme version of a very Neapolitan obsession: the nativity scene. Started in the 15th century, and added to and changed continuously over the next 300 years, it is packed full of figures ranging from angels to a fishmonger, a chestnut seller and a knife grinder. Baby Jesus looks rather non-plussed by all the fuss.

● *Walk through to the end of the gardens for a good view of Castel Nuovo or to the right for an excellent view of the Bay, especially spectacular in the glow of the setting sun.*

! Guiseppe Andreoli, an anatomy professor at Naples University, was told in spring 2002 that parental responsibilities did not cease with age and that he must continue to pay €775 every month to his 30-year old law graduate son until his son was able to find "satisfactory employment".

Napoli nella Raccolta de Mura

piazza Trieste e Trento. *Mon-Sat 0900-1900, Sun 0900-1300. Free. Map 3, E4, p250*

Underground in front of the cafés in piazza Trieste e Trento, this little museum has a collection of posters and other memorabilia from the golden age of Neapolitan song (mostly 1880-1930) as well as some photographs of 'Neapolitan types' from times gone by, such as the macaroni vendor and the straw-bottomed chair mender. Neapolitan songs are constantly piped through the speakers to accompany your visit. If you like this there's more of the same in the Museo dell'Attore Napoletano in piazza Municipio (see p77).

Teatro di San Carlo

piazza Trieste e Trento, **T** 081-7972331/412, www.teatrosancarlo.it *Tours run on Sat and Sun at 1400, 1430, 1500 and 1530. €2.50. Pick up a leaflet at the box office to see the month's programme and prices. Map 3, E5, p250*

Built in eight months in 1737 by Carlo III and partly rebuilt after a fire 79 years later, the luxurious San Carlo Theatre, one of Italy's most prestigious venues, has an interior that's much more magnificent than its slightly anonymous exterior. Opera, ballet and concerts take place here throughout the year and many seats are booked for the entire season by well-off and well-dressed Neapolitans, for whom the place remains the centre of social life. Take a half-hour tour or save up for a performance, and an unashamedly stylish evening (see p182).

Galleria Umberto

Map 3, D4, p250

An enormous palatial cavern of a shopping arcade, the spectacular iron- and glass-domed Galleria is the twin of Galleria Vittorio

Emanuele II in Milan. Built in the 1880s, it is probably a better place to wander through than to shop. A few designer clothes outlets rub shoulders with cheap electrical stores and smart cafés.

Acquedotto Carmignano

From piazza Trieste e Trento, www.lanapolisotterranea.it *Tours last about an hour and a half and run Thu at 2100; Sat 1000, 1200 and 1800; Sun 1000, 1100, 1200 and 1800.* €6. *Map 3, E4, p250*

From *Bar Gambrinus* (probably Naples' most famous café, see p150) on piazza Trieste e Trento you can take a fascinating underground guided tour of the Acquedotto Carmignano, a part of Naples' antique aqueduct network, organized by *Napoli Sotterranea* (Underground Naples, see also p55). The aqueducts date back to Greek and Roman times and remained in use up until a cholera outbreak in the 19th century. Signs point out the exact number of via Chiaia you are under as you pass the private wells of these grand old palazzi. Various drawings, poems and other graffiti still cover many of the walls from the time when many of the tunnels were widened, the floors concreted, and thousands of Neapolitans sheltered (and married and gave birth) down here during the Second World War. Tours are in Italian but it's atmospheric enough to still get a lot out of it without understanding a word.

Castel Nuovo

piazza Municipio, **T** 081-7952003. *Mon-Sat 0900-1930, €5.15. Map 3, D7, p250*

Known locally as the **Maschio Angioino**, the Angevin Strong-hold, both Boccaccio and Petrarch stayed in this sturdy fairytale building. Originally built from stone imported from Mallorca, in the 13th century, it once contained frescoes by Giotto. It was extensively remodelled by the Aragonese in the 15th century, however, and now much of its magic has gone. The **Museo Civico** is on the first and second floors. Guglielmo Monaco's ornate bronze doors, complete with a couple of holes and an embedded cannonball, are worth a look but the collection of Neapolitan paintings is a bit of a mixed bag. More interesting are the chapels downstairs. The tiny Baroque **Cappella delle Anime del Purgatorio** has some slightly alarming frescoes. By way of contrast, the **Cappella Palatina** next door is stark, but has some tantalizing remnants of frescoes by Niccolò Tommaso, and some frustratingly small pieces of Giotto's work next to the tall windows. The **Sala dei Baroni** next door gets its name from the barons murdered here by King Ferrante of Aragon in 1486. Under the pretence of a banquet to settle a dispute, Ferrante lured his victims here and had them arrested and executed. The room was another once frescoed by Giotto, but its only colour now comes from City Council meetings.

● *Without buying a ticket you can still have a look at the impressive Renaissance triumphal arch, built at the entrance to the castle to celebrate the arrival of Alfonso I of Aragon in 1443.*

Castel dell'Ovo
There are also occasional exhibitions held here, especially during Maggio dei Monumenti (see p189). But a good proportion of the castle is either undergoing restoration or given over to office space and may be difficult to gain access to. Map 3, L3/4, p251

Built on a volcanic outcrop into the bay, Castel dell'Ovo is a more intimidating building than its more modern counterpart. The egg of its name was, according to legend, buried on the site by Virgil, who prophesied that when the egg broke Naples would fall.

If you like castles it's worth a wander round, and there are some good views in both directions over Naples and the bay. **Borgo Marinari**, the collection of houses and (mainly) restaurants surrounded by jetties beside the castle, is a popular location that heaves with life on summer evenings but can seem a little deserted out of season.

Centro Storico

*The oldest part of the city is also the most hectic. Scooters, students and street sellers vie for attention with enormous numbers of churches and grand old palazzi. But between the noisy streets a few beautiful **cloisters** provide some welcome respite. The university area is just to the south and in the evenings here, and between piazza del Gesù Nuovo and porta Nilo the scene is boisterous and chaotic. **Piazza Vincenzo Bellini**, just to the north, is a haven of cafés and intellect.*

*Now a UNESCO World Heritage Site, the area still follows the ancient Greek and Roman layout of Neapolis, with three main east-west streets, or decumani. Long, straight **Spaccanapoli** ('Break Naples'), which is made up of via Benedetto Croce, via San Biagio dei Librai and via Vicaria Vecchia, was once the decumanus inferior of the Greek city, while **via dei Tribunali** was the decumanus major. Most of the best sites are on or around these two streets. The ancient decumanus superior of modern-day via Sapienza, via Anticaglia and via Santissimi Apostoli is quieter, plainer and more residential but is still worth a wander.*

▸▸ *See Sleeping p126, Eating and drinking p153, Bars and clubs p172 and Arts and entertainment p177*

 ## Sights

Gesù Nuovo

piazza del Gesù, **T** 081-5518613. *Mon-Sun 0630-1300, 1600-1900. Mass is held in English in the nearby St Francis De Geronimo Hall every Sun and feast day at 1645. Map 2, E2, p248*

Little hint is given of the spectacular interior of this church from its ugly armoured exterior on piazza del Gesù, covered with forbidding grey, pointed, diamond-shaped stones. Indeed the front was originally part of an older 15th-century palazzo on the same site.

★ Spaccanapoli

Tall, dark, though not always handsome, Spaccanapoli cuts a long straight line through the Centro Storico, epitomizing the city with a rich seam of shops, sounds, stalls, smells – and mopeds.

This grand Jesuit construction was designed at the end of the 16th century by Giuseppe Valeriano, and painted and decorated by the best Neapolitan artists of the next 100 years or so, including Solimena, Vaccaro and Fanzago. It continues to be one of the city's most popular and well-used churches. There is such a bewildering collection of beautiful art on the barrel-vaulted ceilings that there is a risk that you may be converted to Catholicism by it, or at least get a cricked neck. The inlaid marble floor and intarsia altars are also worth a good look.

To the right there is a side-chapel dedicated to the local 20th-century doctor and saint Giuseppe Moscati, canonized in 1987, who dedicated himself to the area's poor. Hundreds of ex-votos (including golden syringes) and messages of thanks fill the walls and testify to his enduring popularity.

★ Santa Chiara

via Santa Chiara 49/c. Church: **T** 081-7971235, www.santachiara.org *Mon-Sun 0700-1230, 1600-1900.* Museum/cloister: **T** 081-7971256, www.oltreilchiostro.org *Mon-Sat 0930-1300, 1430-1730, Sun and holidays 0930-1300,* €*4.* *Map 2, E2, p248*

Originally built for Robert of Anjou's wife Sancia di Maiorca in the early 14th century, this complex on the south side of piazza del Gesù suffered a direct hit in the Second World War, and this and the subsequent fire destroyed almost the entire Baroque-decorated interior of the church. It has since been reconstructed in its original Gothic style and it is a rather stark, serious space. Some original features remain, however, notably remnants of a fresco and a tomb from the early 15th century just to the left of the entrance and, in a chapel on the right, the tombs of the Bourbon sovereigns of the city, from Ferdinando I to Francesco II.

However, the 14th-century cloisters are what most come here to see, and rightly so. A beautiful and exceptionally quiet oasis in the midst of all the pandemonium of the Centro Storico, these cloisters are decorated with majolica-tiled seats and columns. Frescoes cover the four walls around the edge while the colourful decorated walkways, with peaceful scenes of rural life, form a cross which divides up the grass and orange trees. Don't sit on the majolica seats though, unless you want a walkie-talkie-wielding attendant bearing down on you rather severely.

In the museum is a well-laid out display of interesting remains salvaged from the bombed-out church as well as some excavations of a Roman swimming pool. Information is only in Italian, however.

● *To the east along Spaccanapoli is Palazzo Filomarino, via Benedetto Croce 12, which was the house of the famous Neapolitan philosopher Croce himself.*

Cappella Sansevero
via de Sanctis 19, **T** 081-5518470. *Mon-Sat 1000-1700 (winter), 1000-1900 summer, Christmas and Easter. Sun 1000-1330. Closed Tue. €5. Map 2, D4, p248*

Built originally around 1590, it is the remodelling of the chapel by the eccentric alchemist and keen experimenter Prince Raimondo di Sangro in the 18th century that makes this chapel worth a visit. Hidden away to the north of piazzetta Nilo, the real highlights of this small but extraordinarily ornate chapel are the allegorical marble sculptures, notably a virtuoso piece, *Disillusion*, by Francisco Queirolo with a figure extricating himself from a net, Antonio Corradini's *Modesty* (a rather immodest nude, but for a particularly thin veil), and an amazingly lifelike *Veiled Christ* by Giuseppe Sanmartino in the centre of the chapel. (The veil on this sculpture seems so life-like and thin that some Neapolitans believe it to be a real body somehow turned to stone by the macabre experiments of Raimondo.) Further evidence of Raimondo's bizarre experiments into preserving human remains can be found downstairs in the chapel, where the petrified veins of two human bodies are conserved in glass cases.

★ Cloisters, Santa Chiara
Wonderfully peaceful, at least until you try to sit on the majolica-tiled seats, Neapolitans come to Santa Chiara's cloisters to read papers on the cool stone benches around the edges.

Cappella e Museo del Monte di Pietà

via San Biagio dei Librai 114. *Weekends only. Sat 0900-1900, Sun 0900-1400. Map 2, D5, p248*

Built between 1597 and 1605 this was originally a Counter-Reformation institution and it has extraordinarily beautiful frescoes to prove it. Rooms to the right of the chapel as you enter the court-yard contain some of the *Banco di Napoli*'s large art collection, but it's the frescoed chapel itself that is more impressive, particularly the ambitious works on a grand scale in the barrel-vaulted nave by Belisario Corenzio illustrating the *Misteri della Passione*.

Via San Gregorio Armeno

Map 2, C5, p248

On via San Gregorio Armeno, running north perpendicular to Spaccanapoli, all year round, shops spill their wares out onto the pavements: thousands upon thousands of figures, some tinier than others, vie for space with models of baskets of fruit, mini electrically pumped water-features and the occasional mechanized man-drinking-beer, or butcher-chopping-meat. Above you angels, suspended from ceilings and doorways, stare down lovingly.

This is the strange world of Naples' **Nativity scenes**, or *presepi*. In the months leading up to Christmas tens of thousands of people come here from all over Italy to stock up for their home cribs, often including pizza-sellers and occasionally politicians and celebrities. If you actually want to be able to walk up and down the street, come at another time of year and take home a very Neapolitan souvenir.

! Originally the purpose of the Monte di Pietà was to give out interest-free loans to fight usury. It is now owned, somewhat ironically, by the *Banco di Napoli*.

"...as for those who say that he who sees a ghost can no longer feel light-hearted, then the same could be said in reverse, for he who returns to thoughts of Naples can never be unhappy."

Goethe, *Journey in Italy*

Chiesa e Chiostro di San Gregorio Armeno

via San Gregorio Armeno 1, **T** 081-5520186. *Mon and Wed-Fri 0900-1200, Tue 0900-1300, Sat and Sun 0900-1230. The cloisters have a separate entrance to the church, up the hill and first left onto via Maffei (the gates at the bottom of the steps are kept locked, ring the bell on the right and someone will let you in).* Map 2, C5, p248

This very baroque little church, complete with a beautiful cloister, is famous in Naples primarily for the remains and the congealed **blood of Santa Patrizia**, which, more generously than her counterpart San Gennaro (see p51), miraculously liquefies every Tuesday. The drawback being that whereas San Gennaro's miracle prevents catastrophes and wins *scudettos* (football champion-ships), this weekly occurrence brings about only babies.

Much of the interior is a little grimy these days, although some of the chapel paintings are superb examples of Neapolitan Baroque, notably those in the first and third chapels on the right, by Pacecco De Rosa and Cesare Fracanzano respectively.

The **San Gregorio Armeno Cloisters**, though similar in peacefulness to those of Santa Chiara, are perhaps not quite as picturesque. What they lack in prettiness, however, they make up for in authenticity – these feel very much like cloisters still in use, from the smiling nun who greets you at the door to the chanting of children from the primary school upstairs which occasionally echoes around the arches ("Ow old are you? Ow old are you?"). Crumbling yellow paint, heavily laden orange trees, and a view of the majol-ica-tiled dome of the church all add to the atmosphere of the place.

Pio Monte della Misericordia

via dei Tribunali 253, **T** 081-446944. *0930-1230 Mon-Sat.* Map 2, B7, p249

Just to the east of via Duomo, this octagonal church, with its grubby exterior, is famous for its extraordinary **Caravaggio**

> ### San Gennaro
>
> Naples' characteristic mix of the sacred, the superstitious, the traditional and the profane is summed up in the phenomenon of San Gennaro, the city's patron saint.
>
> Whatever San Gennaro's miraculous powers were (you can see some stories told on the walls of his chapel in the Duomo), what is important to Neapolitans today (and, they would have you believe, to Italians everywhere), is that his congealed blood miraculously liquefies on cue three times a year: on the Saturday before the first Sunday in May, on 19 September, and on 16 December, just as it has since 1389. His feast day (19 September) is a holiday in Naples, and it's on this day that the San Gennaro hysteria reaches its apex.
>
> Almost anything that can go wrong in Naples (and lots does) can be (and is) put down to the length of time San Gennaro's blood took to liquefy on his last feast day. Mostly though, he seems responsible for the three really important things in life: earthquakes, volcanoes and football.

altarpiece, possibly the city's single most important work of art. The *Seven Acts of Mercy* is an ambitious work on three levels: angels reach down from above while in the middle various Neapolitans engage in merciful acts. At the bottom a sprawled beggar grasps the end of a cloak offered to him by a knight. The scene is typically dark and dramatic and is credited with having done much to enliven Naples' tired mannerist traditions at the beginning of the 17th century. The influence of the work is visible on the left inside the door, where **Caracciolo**'s *Liberation of St Peter* is remarkably similar in composition and style, down to the prostrate figure at the base of the painting, the bare sole of his dirty foot facing out of the painting.

Il Duomo

Duomo: *Mon-Fri 0800-1230, 1630-1900, Sat 0800-1230, 1630-1930, Sun 0800-1330, 1700-1930.* Santa Restituta, Excavations and Baptistery: *Mon-Sat 0900-1200, 1630-1830, Sun 0900-1300. Excavations and Baptistery €2.58. Map 2, A6/7, p248/9*

With such an excess of large spectacular churches in the city, the Duomo is slightly less of a focus here than it might be in other Italian cities. It is still an exceptionally grand building though, and most of the present structure dates from the 13th century. Its chapels are especially interesting, one holding the famous remains of San Gennaro, another being one of the city's oldest buildings. Under the building, in the *Scavi del Duomo*, some fascinating ancient remains have been unearthed.

The **Cappella del Tesoro di San Gennaro** (Chapel of the Treasure of San Gennaro, see p51), painted by artists specially imported from Rome such as Guido Reni, is filled with pictures of various miraculous events in his life, and people's stupefied reactions to them ("See Gennaro fly! See Gennaro escape unscathed from a furnace!" etc). Also here are a number of silver busts of saints, and, hidden behind the altar for most of the year, a silver bust of the man himself, containing his skull, and phials holding his congealed blood.

The **Cripta di San Gennaro** (Crypt) under the altar is an atmospheric place of columns and a kneeling statue of Cardinal Carafa, who rebuilt some of the Duomo destroyed by the 1456 earthquake. The altar contains more of San Gennaro's remains.

The **Cappella di Santa Restituta**, opposite the Chapel of San Gennaro, is actually Naples' oldest surviving basilica. Originally a 4th-century Paleo-Christian structure, it was incorporated into the Duomo when the latter was built. Though transformed after damage suffered in the 1688 earthquake, original columns are still in place, and some excellent ancient frescoes and mosaics remain, especially in the Baptistery. Note that the hours for the chapel match those of the archaeological remains, not the Duomo itself.

As the handout will tell you, the **Scavi del Duomo** (Excavations) are a "hodgepodge" of styles and structures, from Greek times onwards. It's well worth a look though, and in places, especially in the *Itinerario Sinistra* (left-hand itinerary), is quite spectacular.

Highlights down here on Greek and Roman streets include some good bits of Roman mosaic, enormous Greek flagstones, an exceptionally well-constructed and well-preserved rainwater-canal, and, best of all, an intact length of Roman lead pipe running along a drain, with the clearly embossed name "Aurelie Utician". Presumably Mr Utician thought he was advertising his product by stamping his name on it. If he could have proved that 2000 years later his piping would still appear entirely modern and new, he might have had even more success.

The ticket for the excavations also allows you into the Baptistery.

Pinacoteca di Girolamini
via Duomo 142, **T** 081-449139. *Mon-Fri 0930-1250. Free.*
Map 2, B6, p248

A door opposite the Duomo leads to the church of Girolamini, largely unremarkable except that it contains the tomb of Neapolitan philosopher **Giambattista Vico**. To find the much more interesting Pinacoteca di Girolamini, go through the next door up via Duomo. This takes you into a courtyard, from which stairs on the right-hand side lead up to the Pinacoteca.

One of Naples' lesser-known attractions, the Pinacoteca contains an excellent collection of Neapolitan Renaissance paintings. Highlights are three portraits of saints by Jusepe de Ribera (*San Pietro*, *San Paolo* and *San Giacomo Maggiore*) in the end room, a pair of heads (*Testa di Santa* and *Testa del Battista*), one by Massimo Stanzione, one unknown, and, best of all, a beautiful *Sacra Famiglia* by Antonio Viviani. Niccolò de Simone's *Madonna col Bambino* may be the only Madonna you'll see with a moustache. Note that the hours of the Pinacoteca are more flexible than most.

San Paolo Maggiore

piazza San Gaetano, **T** 081-454048. *0900-1300.* Map 2, B5, p248

The steps up to the church of San Paolo Maggiore provide a good view of the piazza and via dei Tribunali below. Inside, an enormous and very grand space opens up. The church was hit by a bomb in the Second World War and despite some attractive frescoes, some of the restoration of the 1603 structure is a little too clean and modern-looking and detracts from the atmosphere of the place. Don't miss the **Sacrestia** (Sacristy) though – a small room to the right of the altar leads to this beautifully decorated space with two 1689-90 works by Francesco Solimena. The two pillars at the front of the church date from the Roman temple of Castor and Pollux, which stood on the same site.

San Lorenzo Maggiore

via dei Tribunali 316, **T** 081-454948. *Mon-Sun 0900-1200, 1700-1900.* Map 2, B6, p248

The slightly severe church is notable for an impressive Gothic chancel, with unusually dense arches and pillars, at the end of the contrastingly plain main apse. The third chapel on the right, with intricate inlaid marble, was built by Fanzago, while the Madonna del Rosario over the alter is by Stanzione. Frescoes in the sixth ambulatory chapel are from the Neapolitan school of Giotto, from around 1334. But perhaps of more interest than the church itself are the excavations underneath (see below).

⬤ *Boccaccio first saw and fell in love with Maria d'Aquino here in 1334 and almost certainly based the character of Fiammetta on her. Fiammetta recurs in many of his works, such as* The Filocolo, L'Elegia di Madonna Fiammetta *and* The Decameron *(see p235).*

Scavi di San Lorenzo Maggiore

piazza San Gaetano 316, **T** 081-2110860. *Mon-Sat 0900-1700, Sun 1000-1330. €4. Map 2, B5, p248*

Under San Lorenzo, an extraordinary and under-appreciated site is still very much work in progress. After buying a ticket and following some photocopied signs ("Scavi") through a maze of scaffolding, you descend into a kind of mini-Pompeii under the centre of Naples. At quiet times you may find yourself completely alone down here, in a remarkably intact cobbled street of ancient Neapolis. As fluorescent lamps flicker on and off above, adding to the slightly unreal atmosphere, you can wander in and out of a bakery, a place for the washing and drying of clothes, and an *aerearium* (where the city's treasure would have been kept). In a covered market at the far end of the excavations, shafts lead up to what would have been the street above. In places, where the excavations have gone a little lower, distinctive Greek tufa bricks are visible from even longer ago.

Occasionally the lamps flicker more off than on, and it can be a bit on the gloomy side, but it's no less fascinating for that. A sheet with a map and guide is provided, but it takes a bit of figuring out.

Napoli Sotterranea

piazza San Gaetano 68, **T** 081-296944, www.lanapolisotterranea.it *Mon-Fri 1200, 1400 and 1600, Thu also 2100, Sat-Sun 1200, 1400, 1600 and 1800. €6.20, plus €2.60 extra for the theatre. See also Acquedotto Carmignano, p41. Map 2, B5, p248*

This tour of Naples' ancient aqueducts, some 30-40 metres under the city, is a fascinating way to appreciate the different layers of history in the city. Originally started by the Greeks, and continued by the Romans, these aqueducts form a web of tunnels under the city, and only a small proportion of the entire network is open to the public. The system was in use up until the cholera epidemic of 1884, and you can see the private supplies of particularly rich

Superstition and Malochio

Naples' 'Cult of Death' may (officially) be a thing of the past, but superstition in general lingers on. Tarot readers are common, and local *Maghi* (magicians) even appear on Neapolitan TV so that people can ring in and ask for *il Malochio* (literally, the bad eye) to be removed from their shoulders, or for it to be put onto others.

families. During the Second World War, thousands of Neapolitans sheltered down here, and uniforms and various wartime finds are on show in one of the caverns you pass through.

An extra tour of the ancient **Roman theatre**, undergoing excavation nearby, is available for payment of a supplement. Slightly bizarrely, you go into somebody's garage, and a bed is pulled aside to reveal a trapdoor leading down to the excavations.

Santa Maria delle Anime del Purgatorio ad Arco
via dei Tribunali, 39. *Mon-Sun 0900-1300. Map 2, C4, p248*

This 17th-century church contains an altar painting by Massimo Stanzione somewhat reminiscent of Caravaggio's *Seven Acts of Mercy* (in nearby Pio Monte della Misericordia) which has been impressively restored. A board by the altar shows the various stages of the cleaning and restoration, from brown to vivid. Stairs lead down to catacombs below and *Napoli Sotterranea* do occasional tours.

The skulls on stone pillars outside this little church are a sign of the supposedly extinct 'cult of the dead', a very Neapolitan tradition, whereby the living would shower gifts onto somebody's bones in exchange for good fortune. The shininess of the skulls' heads, and the number of times they are touched by passers-by suggest the superstitions associated with the cult, if not the cult itself, may be more alive than the church would have you believe.

Piazza Bellini
Map 2, C2, p248

Café life buzzes late into the night in this mostly pedestrianized focus of the city's vaguely alternative community. Piazza Bellini has Naples' only vegetarian restaurant (see p153), its best internet café (see p220) and its most famous literary café (see p155). It also has a sunken area containing some of the original Greek city walls.

Naples

Via Toledo and the Quartieri Spagnoli

*The partly pedestrianized via Toledo (still called via Roma by many, though it hasn't officially been called this for years) is one of Naples' main roads, connecting the two centres of the city and containing many of Naples' high-street shops. It is also a dam, holding back the maze of tiny streets that makes up the Camorra heartland of the **Quartieri Spagnoli** to its west.*

*Towards the Centro Storico, the small sloping **piazza Monteoliveto** has some fine buildings including the Renaissance church of **Sant'Anna dei Lombardi**. Atop a baroque fountain here a youthful Carlo II strikes a rather camp pose. To the north, up the hill from the newly renovated **piazza Dante**, the **Museo Archeologico Nazionale di Napoli** is a treasure trove of mosaics, sculptures, paintings and other finds from southern Italy's antiquity.*

▸▸ *See Sleeping p128, Eating and drinking p156 and Shopping p193*

◉ Sights

Quartieri Spagnoli
Map 3, B/C 2/3, p250

Many Neapolitans will warn you against the Quartieri Spagnoli (literally, Spanish Quarters), seeing it as the city's den of iniquity, and the home of the Camorra. In actual fact, this network of streets running up the hill behind via Toledo is probably as safe as most other areas of Naples: though the locals may occasionally want to shoot each other, they're unlikely to want to harm you.

Built to house Spanish troops in the 16th century and changed very little since, this is now one of Europe's poorest urban areas. There has been much effort to spruce it up since the early 1990s but it remains cramped and economically it struggles, unemployment remaining stubbornly high. It's an atmospheric place to wander around, though, and there are many excellent local restaurants if no obvious sights. At its northern edge, along via Pignasecca to piazza Montesanto is the most interesting part, with some good shops selling household goods and shoes, a market that sells mainly fruit, vegetables and fish and a constant swarm of people shopping, passing through or chatting at the tops of their voices.

★ Sant'Anna dei Lombardi

piazza Monteoliveto 14, **T** 081-5513333. *Mon-Sat 0930-1230. Map 2, G1, p248*

Built in the early part of the 15th century, and an excellent example of the Tuscan influence of the time, the nave of this complex is still in the process of being restored, though work should be completed sometime in 2003. The chapels that have already been restored make it one of the highlights of the city. In the sacrestia Giorgio Vasari's sensuous 16th-century ceiling frescoes illustrating the *Simboli delle Virtù* are some of Naples' most important Renaissance works. The exceptionally skilled inlaid wood panels are attributed to Giovanni da Verona and others (1506-10).

To the right of the entrance to the church (currently reached at the end of a sequence of chapels down the side of the nave) the first chapel contains an excellent bas-relief of the Annunciation on the altar by Benedetto da Maiano. Another chapel has a Pietà by Guido Mazzoni consisting of eight life-size terracotta figures.

La Camorra

Recent scams allegedly involving the Camorra include car cloning: a con whereby the number plate, registration papers and insurance details of a car are copied exactly and sold, often to buyers in the north of Italy. These cloned cars can then avoid paying parking fines and traffic offences. Victims have included Giosue Candita, commander of Naples' traffic police, whose cloned car was collecting him fines in Milan.

More sinisterly, 16 pharmacists were arrested in May 2002 for their part in the Camorra-controlled market in the illegal sale of prescription drugs. And another scam, possibly in allegiance with Colombian cocaine gangs, involves the international sale of faulty second-hand aircraft parts. Arrests were made in Naples in January 2002. The FBI is reported to be looking into possible links with the crash in New York in November 2001 in which 265 people died.

Museo Archeologico Nazionale di Napoli
piazza Museo, 19, **T** 081-4401466, www.marketplace.it/museo.nazionale/ *0900-1900, closed Tue. €6.20.* Map 2, A1, p248

With the finds from Pompeii and Herculaneum alongside other important Roman statues and artefacts, the National Archaeological Museum calls itself the most important museum of archaeology in the world, and it might well be. The sheer breadth and quality of content here is staggering. From enormous grandiose marble statues to small homely paintings, and from erotic oil-lamps to a mosaic made of a million different pieces, the museum gives an amazing idea of the look and feel of the ancient Roman world.

It would be easy to wear yourself out with all this though – if you really want to see it all it's probably worth spreading it over a couple of days. The following should give an idea of some of the highlights. The audio guide, available in English from the ticket office for an extra €4, has some interesting insights, but tends to be a little long-winded, and overly concerned with the history of the collections, rather than with the objects themselves.

It's hard to be prepared for the sheer scale of the **Farnese Marbles**. They are enormous. Of Roman rather than Neapolitan origin, they were brought to Naples by Ferdinand IV. The Farnese Bull, the most famous of them all, is here in its entirety, and a very ambitious piece it is too. Sculpted by Apollonius and Tauriskos in the second century BC, five figures, a dog and a bull represent the myth of Dirce (who was tied to a bull by Zeto and Amphion as punishment for the mistreatment of their mother). Pliny the Elder wrote about this sculpture in his *Natural History*, so we know that it was already considered a masterpiece in ancient times.

The equally large Hercules (looking tired after a hard day's tasking) is probably a reproduction of a bronze Greek statue.

The Farnese statue of Atlas, currently on display upstairs with the Pompeii paintings, has him holding a globe which is covered in the oldest existing symbolic depictions of the constellations and the signs of the zodiac in a form which is generally unchanged today.

The **Roman Mosaics**, many from Pompeii, are extraordinary not just because they seem so modern, but also because they are so well-preserved. The tiny and simple mosaic of two ducks in room LIX is a case in point – it could have been made in almost any period. Two other mosaics by Dioscuride di Sarno in the same room show an extraordinarily accomplished use of the medium. The much-reproduced *Ritratto Femminile* in room LXIV is especially painterly.

It's hard, however, to compete with the vast *Battaglia tra Alessandro e Dario* (Battle between Alexander the Great and Darius, the battle which assured Alexander's conquest of Asia). This colossal mosaic is estimated to contain a million individual *tesserae*, and is approximately 6 m wide and 3 m tall. It is not only the most famous mosaic from antiquity, but is also seen as the most important docu-ment of ancient Greek painting (almost none of which has survived) since it is a copy of a painting from that earlier period.

Of all the collection of **paintings**, the four small and relatively simple female figures from Stabia seem the most powerful. That of Diana, loading an arrow onto a bow, is every bit as beautiful as the much more reproduced Flora.

The *Vaso Blu*, in room LXXXV, an amphora used for wine, is another amazing object. Delicate and ornate cupids in white glass gather and crush grapes against a cobalt blue glass background.

In room LXXXIX a silver bucket from Herculaneum is beautifully illustrated with female figures bathing.

The so-called **Bust of Seneca** in room CXVII turns out not to be of Seneca at all, since a portrait of him was found in 1813 which bears no likeness to the bust. But more than 40 copies have been found, so the subject's fame is not in doubt, even if his identity still is.

The **Farnese Bowl** is considered one of the finest pieces of cameo ever made. Made at the Egyptian Ptolemaic Court it was transferred to Rome after Octavius's victory over Cleopatra. Since then it has also been a treasure of the Byzantine court, the court of Frederick II, the Persian court, the Aragonese court, the Medici family and the Farnese family.

The scale **model of Pompeii** isn't quite as good as being there, but it does give a good idea of the size of the city (though the eastern part of the city, including the amphitheatre, is missing from the model). It's also an impressive work in its own right. It was constructed in exceptional detail (in places including tiny reproductions of frescoes) between 1861 and 1864.

Of the museum's collection of erotica, now in the **Gabinetto Segreto**, Francesco I, king of Naples from 1825-1830, declared "it would be as well to confine all the obscene objects in one room... the only people allowed to visit this room being of mature age and proven morality". The official attitude towards this infamous collection has wavered over the years, from embarrassed to moralistic. The 'Secret Room' was opened by Garibaldi when he entered the city – the way was administered by the Bourbons having come to be seen as backward and repressed. It was semi-closed again by Mussolini's fascist regime. Today, on the surface, the position has not changed too much since Francesco's day: you need to book a reservation when you buy your ticket (these are free), and you're only allowed in with a guide. Actually, though, the guided tour is fascinating, and the attitude more educational than puritanical.

The most striking thing about the collection is not its eroticism but its variety. The multitudinous uses of the phallus include bells, oil lamps and symbols of prosperity to hang outside one's shop. Figures of men with enormous penises carrying serving trays were apparently a joke at the expense of focaccia-sellers, and some of the erotic paintings were probably prostitutes' adverts.

The collection's most famous piece, that of Pan making love to a goat, is, as the guide will probably point out with a completely straight face, beautifully and delicately sculptured. Other highlights include a shop sign portraying a donkey sodomizing a lion and being crowned by victory, and a simple depiction of an erect phallus, under which is written "Here lives happiness".

Corso Umberto I and around

*Corso Umberto I, the rettifilo (straight line), runs southwest from the ugly (but pretty much unavoidable) transport hub of piazza Garibaldi to piazza Giovanni Bovio, and is a soulless thoroughfare, almost always busy with traffic. To the north is the **university**, with small but interesting museums; to the south the Mercato district, stretching down to via Nuova Marina and the industrial port area, is a claustrophobic residential area, punctuated by shops selling mattresses and toilet rolls, though it has an extraordinarily lively market at **Porta Nolana**.*

*The **Fontana Medina**, in piazza Bovio, complete with Neptune and satyrs (and sea-monsters courtesy of Pietro Bernini) at the end of the 16th century, was, at the time of writing, hidden behind hoardings as the construction of a new metro station continues.*

▸▸ *See Sleeping p130 and Shopping p193*

Sights

★ Mercato di Porta Nolana
Map 2, D12, p249

Just to the west of the Circumvesuviana Terminal this extraordinary piece of Neapolitan theatre spills out every morning around Porta Nolana onto via Cesare Carmignano and via Sopramuro. It's a heady mix of shellfish (under arcs of constantly spraying water), fruit and veg, pirated CDs, DVDs and software, bread, olives, enormous live octopuses (still writhing as they are chopped up), contraband cigarettes, every kind of fish imaginable, extraordinarily cheap beer, toy helicopters and fishing rods, overlaid with bellowed Neapolitan dialect, and loud Italian pop music. Not to be missed.

Piazza Mercato
Map 2, E10, p249

Despite its contemporary use as a car park, piazza Mercato has previously been the stage for some of Naples' most dramatic history. Site for public executions, including those at the end of the failed Parthenopean Republic (see History, p226), it was also the point where Masaniello's 1647 uprising started, the fish vendor leading a violent revolt against a Spanish fruit tax. Naples' plague also began here in 1656, killing as much as three-quarters of the city's population.

The piazza has one of the area's few landmarks, the ancient church of **Santa Maria del Carmine**, restructured at the end of the 13th century, with an imposing façade and a 75-metre bell-tower decorated at the top with majolica tiles, added in the 17th century. Annually on 16th July a popular firework display from the campanile marks the feast of the Madonna del Carmine.

● *Santa Maria del Carmine has a crucifix which supposedly ducked to avoid a cannonball in Alfonso of Aragon's 1439 attack on the city.*

I Musei dell'Università

Anthropology, Mineralogy, Zoology, via Mezzocannone 8,
Paleontology, largo San Marcellino 10, www.musei.unina.it,
T 081-2535162. *Mon-Fri 0900-1330, Sat-Sun 0900-1300. Ticket covers
all museums, and is valid on different days, €1.50   Map 2, F5, p248*

Comprising the museums of zoology, anthropology, palaeontology
and mineralogy, this collection (officially the "Naples University
Interdepartmental Museums") is very effectively hidden deep in the
depths of the university, though there are signs from the via
Mezzocannone entrance. Also, the museums are rather old-
fashioned, and not especially pertinent to the city itself. There are
some fascinating exhibits though, and, if you can find them, they're
worth a wander round. Information is given, but generally in Italian.
If you're lucky you'll find a guide willing to do a tour in English.

The Mineralogy Museum is particularly grand, and has an
interesting room with an amazing variety of different pieces of
lava. The Zoology Museum is pretty much as you would imagine it
was 100 years ago: lots of stuffed animals, a life-size model of a
hippo, and skeletons of an elephant and a couple of whales. The
Anthropology Museum is small but has some unusual exhibits,
including a beautiful carved bone, and a skeleton from Pompeii.
The Palaeontology Museum is in a recently restored convent.

La Sanità and Capodimonte

*Heading north from the centre of the city you climb ever upwards
along via Toledo, which goes through several name changes before
reaching the hillside* **Parco di Capodimonte***, a green escape above
and behind the city, with Naples' greatest and biggest art collection,
including important paintings by Caravaggio, Titian, Raphael,
Brueghel and Botticelli, in the* **Palazzo Reale***.*

*Below the hill of Capodimonte, La Sanità is another of the city's
down-at-heel areas, but also has some fascinating ancient catacombs*

*with Paleo-Christian mosaics and frescoes: the **Catacombe di San Gennaro** and the **Catacombe di San Gaudioso**. In the **Cimitero delle Fontanelle** (closed for renovation at the time of writing), anonymous skulls are traditionally 'adopted' by the living in hope of receiving good fortune from the souls of the dead.*

*Further east, along the busy via Foria, the **Orto Botanico** (botanical garden) is a rare oasis of greenery and peace.*

▸▸ *See Sleeping, p132*

◉ Sights

Parco di Capodimonte
Bus 24 runs from outside Galleria Umberto I via piazza Municipio and piazza Dante up to La Sanità and Capodimonte, but can be rather infrequent. Map 6, A3, p256

Originally created as a hunting ground for Carlo III, the park is now popular as a weekend excursion from the city, and can become a little overrun, especially around the Palazzo Reale itself, where countless games of football take place on the worn grass between the palm trees. The views of the city and the bay to the south are spectacular from here, but it's as the park stretches north that you are more likely to find some peace away from the crowds.

Palazzo Reale di Capodimonte
*via Capodimonte, **T** 081-7499111. Tue-Sat 1000-1900, Sun 0900-1400, closed Mon. €7.50, €6.50 (1400-1700). Gabinetto dei Disegni e Stampe: Tue-Sat 0940-1400.* Map 6, C2, p256

Rather grander than the hunting lodge Carlo III apparently originally wanted, this imposing scarlet palace on top of the hill, begun in 1738, is home to the Farnese Collection of Renaissance art (which Carlo inherited from his mother Elisabetta, the last of the Farnese) alongside the Bourbon Collection and a great number of the most important Neapolitan works from the 14th century onwards. In case this doesn't impress you enough, there is a floor of modern art, and some elaborately decorated royal apartments.

It's the art that most come to see, however. This is one of the world's great collections, large and broad enough to satisfy the most ardent fans of Renaissance and post-Renaissance art, and with enough gems to convert just about everybody else.

To try and see everything in one go is probably over-ambitious. The first two floors alone comprise 160 rooms and that's before you've looked at any modern art, photography, drawings or prints. A half-day could easily be spent just looking at the highlights; the following are some suggestions of where to start.

On the first floor, the **Farnese Collection** starts at the top of the stairs and proceeds all the way down the side of the building. In here are some of the most obvious highlights in the museum, starting with Raphael and Titian's various portraits of Pope Paolo III from youth to old age in room 2, and Masaccio's *Crucifixion* in room 3. Also in these first few rooms is Vasari's ambitious *Allegory of Justice, Truth and Vice*.

Titian's *Danae* (room 11) is possibly the highlight of the first floor, however: the naked Danae is seduced by Jupiter who rains down gold upon her. It is an extraordinarily erotic painting, especially given that it was painted for the private chambers of a Cardinal. In the same room, El Greco's *Soflon* is a small but extraordinarily modern, almost impressionist, piece.

Other paintings worth looking out for on the first floor include Botticelli's early *Madonna with Child and Two Angels* (room 6), Parmigianino's *Portrait of a Young Woman* (which the museum seems to have adopted as its symbol, perhaps because of the powerfully fixating look in the girl's eyes), two allegorical Brueghels in room 17, Caracci's showpiece *The Mystic Marriage of St Catherine* (room 19), and Guido Reni's dramatic *Atalanta and Hippomenes* in room 22.

The **Royal Apartments**, filled with period furniture,

▶ Il Lotto

The lottery is already big news in Italy. In Naples it is elevated to an importance almost alongside Padre Pio, Maradona and San Gennaro. *Il Lotto* is a lottery consisting of 90 numbers, and in the Neapolitan lottery player's *La Smorfia*, each number is equated to a dream. Go along to *un banco di lotto* with your dreams and the ticket seller will interpret their meaning for you, and help you pick your numbers.

Particular meanings range from the poetic (2: little girl, 76: fountain, 45: good wine) to the mundane (42: coffee, 68: soup), from the strange (85: souls of Purgatory, 48: dead man talking) to the downright rude (28: 'tits', 16: 'bum', 29: 'cock', and 6: 'That which you see inside').

Capodimonte ceramics and paintings (including an oddly out-of-place Renoir), are all on this floor too.

Don't wear yourself out before the climb up to the **second floor**, however, because this is the museum's real highlight. Don't miss Titian's beautiful *Annunciation*, which has a room (75) all to itself, or Caldara's series of six darkly expressionistic panels, but even these pale slightly in comparison with what's to follow.

Originally commissioned by the De Franchis family for the family chapel in San Domenico Maggiore but now hanging in pride of place at the end of a long corridor of galleries, Caravaggio's *Flagellation* is an extraordinary composition. Savagely violent and dramatic, the large dark space above the figures gives an oppressive feel to the image, while the crouching figure bottom left lends a sense of depth as well as an almost cinematic feeling of impending brutality. Actually depicting the moment immediately prior to Christ's flagellation, Caravaggio's very human drama puts into perspective the detached religiosity visible in much of the rest of the museum.

In everything that comes after, you tend to see Caravaggio's influence, especially in the works of Battistello and his Neapolitan contemporaries. These rooms go on and on, and you'll need stamina to keep going, though Artemesia Gentileschi's *Susanna Washing* is well worth a look, as are her *Judith* and *Holofernes*, Stanzione's *Martyring of Saint Agatha*, and Ribero's *Maddalena in Meditation*.

On the **third floor**, a more eclectic mix of painting and photography eventually gives way to a space filled with some interesting modern art including an Andy Warhol pop art depiction of the explosion of Vesuvius.

Back on the ground, the **Gabinetto dei Disegni e Stampe** (Drawing and Prints) has some interesting works, including a Rembrandt and a Tintoretto.

Catacombe di San Gaudioso

piazza della Sanità, **T** 081-483238 www.cib.na.cnr.it/vergini/visitacat.html   *Tours only (about 40 mins), Mon-Sun 0930, 1015, 1100, 1145, 1230, also Sat 1710, 1750, 1830. €3.   Map 6, F2, p256*

Bang in the middle of La Sanità, under the cavernous church of Santa Maria della Sanità, these rather dank and mouldy catacombs are notable for their rare 5th- and 6th-century Paleo-Christian mosaics and frescoes. Taking up most of the space here, however, are modifications made by Dominican monks in the 17th century, when the church above was also built. They took up the unhealthy Aragonese habit of seating dead bodies in *seditori*, stone seats where the bodies were left to decompose and the bones dry out before being moved to a communal *ossarium* or private tomb. They also set the skulls of the dead into the walls and painted skeletons around them. Many of these can still be seen.

Catacombe di San Gennaro

via Capodimonte 16, **T** 081-7411071. *Map 6, D1, p256*

Up towards Capodimonte, these catacombs contain even earlier frescoes from the second century AD, and became an important pilgrimage site in the fifth century when San Gennaro's body was moved here from Pozzuoli. The catacombs were closed at the time of writing, but are due to reopen soon.

Orto Botanico
via Foria 223, **T** 081-449759. *Mon-Fri 0900-1400, theoretically by appointment only, though it may be possible to slip in. Free.*
Map 6, E6, p256

Stepping up into this oasis from the hectic via Foria below is quite a contrast, not to say a relief. Wide open paths wind around the site with tall palms and a variety of other trees and plants, all well labelled. Founded by Joseph Bonaparte in 1807 the garden concentrates on Mediterranean flora. There are pristine lawns and the fern section is particularly impressive. To the east of the gardens are the crumbling remains of Carlo III's 18th-century **Albergo dei Poveri**, built to house the city's poor. Covering 103,000 square metres it is still Europe's biggest public building, though only a fifth of the original plan was ever completed. It's currently being restored at vast expense.

Chiaia, Mergellina and Posillipo

*Head west from piazza del Plebiscito along the increasingly smart via Chiaia and you will find yourself in **piazza dei Martiri**, a focus point for the more up-market end of town which starts here and swings around through Chiaia along the Rada Caracciolo seafront to the yacht-filled marina and port of Mergellina and up the hill to Posillipo.*

*Chiaia is an area for wandering, shopping, eating and sitting at cafés watching the world go by. By night, life becomes more energetic as many of the city's smarter clubs and bars open their doors and well-dressed and wealthy young Naples spills out onto the streets among the potted plants. Surrounded by expensive 18th- and 19th-century residences, there is a park (**Villa Comunale**) with an* *aquarium, and a villa with a museum and gardens (**Villa Pignatelli**).*

*Along the seafront there's even a beach of sorts and the sea seems more present here than in the rest of the city – you can walk along beside it all the way from Castel dell'Ovo to the attractive **Porticciolo di Mergellina** (marina of Mergellina), where a cluster of restaurants and cafés creates a bustling atmosphere.*

*By the time you start to climb the hill into Posillipo, residential becomes presidential, and as the coast road heads southwest, much of the sea itself is unattainable at the bottom of very smart gardens and private drives. There are still occasional bits of coast you can reach along this exclusive stretch however, notably at **Marechiaro**.*

▸▸ *See Sleeping p133, Eating and drinking p158 and Bars and clubs p172*

◉ Sights

Villa Comunale
May-Oct 0700-0000, Nov-Apr 0700-1000. Tram: 1 or 4.
Map 4, L1-7, p253

The city's biggest sea-level green space, this long park has a handsome bandstand, curving paths, palm trees, a long, wide paved avenue, clover, daisies and even some swings. Busy roads on either side do their best to spoil the peace, however, and this is more a place to promenade than to sunbathe. Attempts to sit on the grass may result in park wardens on bicycles ringing their bells and shaking their fingers at you.

Halfway along the park, across the road a dirty **beach** connects the seafront to a breakwater. However, the quantity of broken glass should put you off swimming before you even start to think about the cleanliness of the water. But the breakwater provides excellent views of the bay, and isn't a bad place to sit, picnic and sunbathe.

★ Mergellina marina

Expensive yachts and decrepit fishing boats: the Mergellina marina is as expansive as the Centro Storico is cramped.

Acquario

Villa Comunale 1, via Caracciolo, **T** 081-5833111. *Tue-Sat 0900-1800, Sun 0930-1900. €1.50.   Map 4, L4/5, p253*

In the middle of the Villa Comunale, one of Europe's oldest aquariums (perhaps even the oldest) is a centre of scientific study as well as a visitor attraction, and has over 200 species from the Bay of Naples. At the time of writing it was closed for renovation.

● *The liberating forces in 1944 were given a banquet which reputedly included the entire edible population of the aquarium.*

Villa Pignatelli

Riviera di Chiaia, **T** 081-7612356. *Tue-Sun 0830-1400. €3.87.   Map 4, J3/4, p253*

This grand villa, built in the 1820s, once belonged to the Rothschild family and was given to the Italian state in 1952. It has beautiful gardens as well as some magnificent rooms on the ground floor. Upstairs it contains the Banco di Napoli collection in the **Museo Principe Aragona Pignatelli Cortes**, a somewhat patchy selection of art from the Renaissance to the 20th century. The highlight is probably Gaspare Traversi's comic 18th-century composition *The*

Secret Letter. An 18th-century Gaspar van Wittel scene looking west over Chiaia is fascinating, but not for artistic reasons.

Porticciolo di Mergellina
Map 5, L5, p255

The marina at the western end of via Caracciolo is an absorbing mix of smart yachts and tiny fishermen's boats, and a great place for the evening passeggiata, with an excellent view of the city, Vesuvius, and, on a clear day, the whole of the Bay of Naples round to Capri. You can walk right out to the end of the breakwater and sit among the fishermen and lovers watching the city and Vesuvius turn more and more orange in the light of the setting sun.

● *The chalets, on the other side of the road from the marina, are a popular place to come for coffee, cakes and ice-cream.* Chalet Ciro *is the most famous, and has amazing cakes, but nearby* Chiquitos *does especially good ice-cream and has much smaller queues.*

Parco Vergiliano a Piedigrotte
Salita della Grotta 20, Mergellina, **T** 081-669390. *Mon-Sun 0900-1hr before sunset. Free. Map 5, K2, p255*

Under the railway bridge to the left of the attractive church of Santa Maria di Piedigrotte, this park is a little oasis in the midst of traffic chaos, not to be confused with the Parco Virgiliano at the far western end of Posillipo. The tomb of the rather more recent poet Giacomo Leopardi (who died in a cholera outbreak in 1837) is also here, half way up. Of more interest is the **Crypta Neapolitana**, the world's longest Roman road tunnel, which connected Naples to Pozzuoli and Baia. It's closed but you can stare past the detritus to daylight at the far end, 603 m away. Steps up and around the top of the tunnel lead to **Virgil's Tomb**, a strangely shaped building resembling a giant beehive. Whether it actually contains the his remains seems to be open to question, but you won't hear many Neapolitans denying it.

Marechiaro

Bus 140 from Mergellina to the top of via Marechiaro, then a 20 minute walk down the hill, or catch rather infrequent bus 11.

This attractive collection of houses and restaurants by the seafront at Marechiaro has a romantic and villagey feel, and is certainly a different world from central Naples. Unless you're hungry though, there's not much to do except sit by the sea and look at the view.

Vomero

*On the hill directly behind the city centre is Vomero, a newer area of town, with decent shops and a good park in **Villa Floridiana**. Its main attractions are older, however: the **Castel Sant'Elmo** and the monastery of the **Certosa di San Martino**, with its excellent museum, overlook the city from a spectacular position . Just to the south of the shopping area, the Villa Floridiana is a shady park and home to the **Museo Nazionale della Ceramica Duca di Martina**. It's slightly cooler than in the city up here, and isn't a bad place for a picnic, though manic football games may disturb your peace a little.*

▸▸ *See Sleeping p135, Eating and drinking p162 and Shopping p193*

◉ Sights

★ Certosa di San Martino

largo San Martino 5, **T/F** 081-5781769. *Tue-Sat 0830-7.30, Sun 0900-1930, closed Mon. €6. All of the city's funiculars go up to Vomero, but they tend to centre on piazza Vanvitelli. You can walk from any of them to the Certosa, or catch buses C31, C32 or V1 from piazza Vanvitelli. Bus C30 runs from piazza Garibaldi.* Map 4, C8, p252

Recently restored, the Certosa di San Martino began life as a Carthusian monastery in the 14th century. It now contains (and is often referred to as) the excellent **Museo di San Martino**, and is one of Naples' most satisfying sights. For the one ticket, you get some good paintings, an elegant cloister, an exhibition of *presepi* (nativity scenes), one of Naples' most spectacular churches, extraordinary views, terraced gardens, entrance to the Castel Sant'Elmo next door and even a Cinderella-style carriage.

The **church** is decorated as richly as any other in the city, from the floor to the ceiling and including everything in between. Paintings by Ribera, Stanzione, Vaccaro and others adorn the main space. Equally impressive are the other rooms to the left and right (the entrances hidden behind the altar). The Sacrestia has amazing inlaid wood panels, and Flaminio Torelli's *Presentazione al Tempio* in the Passetto tra Capitolo e Parlatorio is just one example of many more fine paintings. There are even signs to tell you what's what.

The **main cloister** is reached through a long high corridor built by Fanzago. Most of the museum exhibits surround this space.

The *Quarto del Priore* contains Renaissance and pre-Renaissance works, including a beautiful marble statue of the *Madonna con Bambino e San Giovannino* by Bernini, and a painting of San Lorenzo by Caracciolo, clearly showing Giotto's influence.

● *At the western end of this section you can wander down through the rather plain terraced gardens, with Naples spread out below. At the other end a balcony gives a good view of the rest of the city to Vesuvius.*

Even more interesting is the section *Immagini e Memorie della Città*, in which paintings and maps of Naples at various stages through history are juxtaposed with views of the contemporary version out of the windows. The highlight here is probably the anonoymous *Tavola Strozzi*, considered a reliable depiction of the city in the 15th century because of the accurate representation of

! The *Parlatorio* (talking-place) is so-called because it was here that monks could have their rare moments of communication.

buildings that still stand today, including the Castel Nuovo, and the Certosa itself.

Castel Sant'Elmo

via Tito Angelini 22, **T** 081-5784030. *0900-1900, closed Mon. €1. A ticket to the Certosa also allows entry to the castle. See the Certosa (above) for details of how to get there. Map 4, C7, p252*

Castel Sant'Elmo, despite its size and prominent position, visible from much of the city, suffers slightly in comparison with its neighbour. It has stood here, in some form or other since the 14th century, and in its current shape since the 16th century. Its only problem is that it's hard to see much of it.

Under normal circumstances access is only to the roof (piazza d'Armi), and though the view is spectacular there's not too much else to see. However, the first floor is often opened for exhibitions, allowing access to the interior of the restored castle.

● *As an alternative to public transport, the steps of* Pedamentina a San Martino *(which predate the funicular railways) wind down from the piazza outside the Castle and Certosa to corso V Emanuele. Cross this road and a couple more bends will take you to the western end of Spaccanapoli, and down into the Centro Storico. Recommended more on the way down than the way up.*

Villa Floridiana

0830-1 hour before sunset. Map 4, E2, p252

One of Naples' few true parks, the Villa Floridiana has trees, shady paths, no scooters, lovers, joggers, and even some grass. At the time of writing the lower part of the park was closed for restoration, which hopefully won't take too long since this is where the best views down over Naples are from.

Museo Nazionale della Ceramica Duca di Martina

Villa Floridiana, **T** 081-5788418. *Tue-Sun entrance only at 0930, 1100 and 1230. Closes at 1400. €2.50. Funicolare di Chiaia and Funicolare Centrale both terminate close to the entrance to the park: from either walk down via Cimarosa to reach the entrance. Head downhill and right through the park to find the museum.* Map 4, G2, p253

The Duca di Martina National Ceramic Museum, in what was once a royal villa (given to his mistress and second wife the Duchess of Floridiana by King Ferdinando in 1815) in the Villa Floridiana, has some good pieces of oriental and Italian ceramics and could be an excellent museum but is currently held back by a strange opening policy (presumably due to lack of funding) which only allows the public in at three points during the day.

The basement holds the oriental collection, with good information in English as well as Italian and lots of priceless vases. Some of the plainer Edo vases in blue and white are especially beautiful.

The ground floor has a somewhat eclectic mix of glass, ivory, boxes and some very attractive 16th-century majolica pottery.

Upstairs is more recent (mainly 18th-century) porcelain including pieces from the royal dinner service, much of which may be overly ornate for some tastes.

⭐ **Museums, galleries and churches**

Museums

Museo Archeologico Nazionale di Napoli (National Archeological Museum) Enormous collection of finds from Pompeii, Herculaneum and the rest of the Roman Empire, p59.

Museo di San Martino (Museum of San Martino) Ex-monastery with church, cloister, gardens, paintings and great views, p74.

Museo di Palazzo Reale (Royal Palace Museum) Sumptuous royal apartments, theatre and chapel, p38.

Museo Principe Aragona Pignatelli Cortes (Prince Aragona Pignatelli Cortes Museum) Gardens, ballroom and 17th-19th-century Neapolitan art, p71.

Museo Nazionale della Ceramica Duca di Martina (Duke of Martina Ceramic Museum) Neapolitan ceramics, mostly in the ornate Capodimonte style, p76.

Museo Civico di Castel Nuovo (Civic Museum of Castel Nuovo) Chapels, meeting rooms, grand halls, art and bronze doors in Naples' second castle, p41.

Musei di Antropologia, Mineralogia, Zoologia e Paleontologia della Università (University Museums of Anthropology, Mineralogy, Zoology and Paleontology) Old fashioned museums with stuffed animals and glass cases, p64.

Napoli nella Raccolta De Mura (Napoli in the De Mura Collection) Small piece of nostalgia for the golden age of Neapolitan song, p40.

Museo dell'Attore Napoletano (Museum of Neapolitan Actors), piazza Municipio, **T** 081-4203331. *Mon-Sat 0900-1900, Sun 0900-1300. Free.* More nostalgia, this time for Neapolitan theatre and actors.

Museo, Scavi e Chiostro di Santa Chiara (Museum, Archeological Site and Cloister of Santa Chiara) Beautiful, tiled cloisters with a museum and some excavations attached, p44.

★ **Galleries**

Gallerie e Museo Nazionali di Capodimonte (Capodimonte Gallery and Museum) Fine (and enormous) collection of mainly Renaissance art, p65.

Pinacoteca di Girolamini (Gallery of the Girolamini) Underrated collection of Neapolitan paintings off a tree-filled cloister, p53.

L'Archivio Fotografico Parisio (Parisio Photographic Archive) Interesting photographic archive of the city, p38.

Accademia di Belle Arti (Academy of Arts), via Santa Maria di Costantinopoli 107, **T** 081-441887. Paintings, sculptures and etchings in an ex-convent.

Churches, chapels and catacombs

Cappella Sansevero (Sansevero Chapel) Baroque chapel with amazing marble statues and macabre remains, p46.

Catacombe di San Gennaro Frescoed Paleo-Christian tombs from as long ago as the second century AD, p68.

Catacombe di San Gaudosio Ancient skulls and bizarre burial rituals under La Sanità, p68.

Duomo (Cathedral) Cathedral with two interesting chapels and the remains of San Gennaro, p52.

Pio Monte della Misericordia Small church with striking Caravaggio altarpiece, p50.

Sant'Anna dei Lombardi Church complex with exquisite Vasari frescoes and some impressive terracotta statues, p58.

Gesù Nuovo Fresco-adorned church with ugly exterior, p43.

San Gregorio Armeno Neapolitan baroque in the church holding the remains of St Patricia, p50.

San Francesco di Paola Neoclassical dome which dominates the focal point of piazza del Plebiscito, p35.

Around the Bay of Naples 81 A once-beautiful coastline hides staggering amounts of history, at Pompeii and Herculaneum for starters, amid 60 years of thoughtless development. Get through the industrial sprawl, and there are still pockets of natural charm on the Sorrento Peninsula.

The islands 97 Ischia has thermal spas, a spectacular castle, an ex-volcano and several thousand German tourists. Capri, dotted with caves and smart villas, is more cosmopolitan and perhaps the most refined. Flatter, smaller Procida is the most Italian and still depends on its fishing industry as much as its tourists.

Amalfi Coast 110 Amalfi itself is the most famous attraction, but Positano to the west and Ravello, inland up the mountainside, are even more picturesque. And then, of course, there's the sea.

Further afield 118 At Paestum, wild flowers entwine themselves around three majestic temples and the remnants of a Greek, and subsequently Roman, city. Caserta endeared itself to Charles III of Bourbon, so he built a grand royal palace here.

Around the Bay of Naples

Pompeii and Herculaneum are generally top of people's Roman lists, but the area also has the sunken and crumbling mysteries of Pozzuoli, Baia and Cuma to extend the ancient theme. Parts of the Sorrento Peninsula remain wonderfully wild or languorously agricultural and Sorrento itself is atypical of the bay, wrapped up in its own cosier world. And then of course there's smouldering Vesuvius watching over the drama below and wondering what to do next.

Pompeii, Herculaneum and Vesuvius

Towering to the east of Naples, **Vesuvius** *is a constant presence and climbing to its top is an impressive experience. Its victims from nearly 2000 years ago,* **Pompeii**, **Herculaneum**, *and* **Oplontis** *form a one-off exhibit of the Roman world stopped in its tracks.*

The well-known attractions of Pompeii and Vesuvius tend to overshadow (the latter literally) Herculaneum, perhaps unjustly. Much less visited, again perhaps unfairly, are the **Villa Poppaea** *at Oplontis and the remains at Stabia (Castellmare). All are fascinating, though without Vesuvius they would be remembered merely (if at all) as more old Roman remains in an area with plenty of old Roman remains.*

Sights

Pompeii
T 081-8575347, www.pompeiisites.org *Apr-Oct 0830-1930, last entrance 1800. Nov-Mar 0830-1700, last entrance 1530. €8.26, including same-day visits to Oplontis, Stabia and Boscoreale. See Getting around p25 and p26.*

Herculaneum and Oplontis have their fans but there's a reason that Pompeii is the most famous of Vesuvius' victims. It may not be as luxurious as Oplontis or as well-preserved as Herculaneum, but the sheer scale of Pompeii is staggering. Here is an entire Roman town, once home as many as 20,000 people, ruined yes, but in many ways extraordinarily intact.

The main problem may be deciding what to see, or exhaustion after having tried to see everything. The fact that many of the site's best houses are often closed is perhaps a blessing in disguise – at least some of these decisions are made for you. Much of the wonder of the place is to be had simply by wandering around, looking into ordinary houses that even the most complete guidebooks don't mention. Some of the most affecting parts are the most ordinary: tracks on the roads where carts have worn down the stones, shop signs advertising their wares, simple mosaics warning you to "beware of the dog". The following are some of the many highlights.

★ Pompeii
Amphorae, chunks of columns, pieces of pottery and plaster versions of one-time inhabitants of Pompeii sit gathering dust not far from where they were found.

Forum

After entering through Porto Marina, the first big space you come to is the Forum. This was the centre of public life in the city and the main temples (such as the **Temple of Apollo** and the **Temple of Jupiter**) are based around it. In the (Roman) public toilets to the northwest, amphorae and other finds are piled high on shelves as well as casts of the dead, whose bodies rotted away, leaving moulds in the solidified ash into which plaster was poured by excavators.

Forum Thermal Baths

To the north of the Forum, this baths complex was the only one still in use after the earthquake of 62AD. It is divided into men's and women's sections, each containing a frigidarium, tepidarium and calidarium. The men's tepidarium is particularly well-preserved, with rows of plaster figures which seem to hold up the barrel-vaulted ceiling.

House of the Tragic Poet

North of the Thermal Baths, the House of the Tragic Poet is most notable for the mosaic in its doorway: under a picture of a chained dog it warns you: *cave canem* (beware of the dog).

House of the Faun

Further north, on vicolo di Mercurio, is one of Pompeii's most famous and elegant houses, the House of the Faun. This is a grand villa, and must have been home to some of Pompeii's most important citizens. Its two most important finds, the dancing bronze statue of a faun and the gigantic million-tessera mosaic of the Battle of Issos, are in the Museo Archeologico in Naples, though a copy of the faun is here.

House of the Vetti

Possibly Pompeii's most popular attraction, the House of the Vetti, near the House of the Faun on vicolo dei Labirinto, is an excellently preserved treasure trove of Pompeian painting. Much of the sumptuous decoration here is from the period after the earthquake of 62AD. The exceedingly well-endowed figure of Priapus in the doorway symbolized fertility and also served to ward off evil spirits. Inside frescoes depict mythological scenes such as Ixion being tied to a wheel by Hephaestus as punishment for having looked at Zeus's wife and Dionysus waking Ariadne. A frieze running around the walls depicts cupids busy selling perfume, gathering grapes and doing target practice. Erotic panels decorating the servants' quarters have led to questions about the role of servants in the Roman world. At the time of writing the house was closed for restoration.

House of Venus

The beautiful and astonishingly well-preserved fresco here of Venus riding in a shell through the waves accompanied by cupids predates Botticelli's more famous version by about one and a half thousand years.

★ Small theatre (Odeon)

Pompeii's semi-circular small theatre, or Odeon, is more complete than its bigger neighbour, the Large Theatre, and is an extremely beautiful space which would have been used for mime, plays and musical events.

● *The Odeon has very particular acoustics: if you stand on the grey stone in the middle of the stage, equidistant from the ends of the seating, and talk, you will have the extremely strange sensation of being in a very small room, with your voice bouncing back at you.*

Villa dei Misteri

Outside the city walls, this large country villa has Pompeii's best-preserved fresoes: an extraordinary cycle depicting the initiation of a girl into the cult of Dionysus. At the time this cult was banned by Rome but remained popular, especially in the south of Italy.

City walls

A walk around the outside of the city walls enables you to escape the crowds and take in Pompeii from a different angle. There is also plenty to see here: the gates to the city and some impressive tombs.

Amphitheatre

Holding approximately 12,000 people and built around 80BC, this is one of the oldest Roman amphitheatres, and may have been used as a model for others. It held gladiatorial combats, as well as events such as the recreation of great sea battles. Unlike some modern stadiums it had a velarium, or cover, which could be stretched across in case of rain.

● *At one point, after riots between fans of Pompeii and Nuceria, the Roman senate banned games here for 10 years.*

Oplontis

via Sepolcri 1, Torre Annunziata **T** 081-8621755. *Apr-Oct 0830-1930, last entry 1800; Nov-Mar 0830-1700, last entry 1530. €5, or see Herculaneum, p86, for details of combined tickets. From the front of station (Torre Annunziata) turn left, then right at the end of the road. It's a five-minute walk. See Getting around, p26*

It is thought that Nero's second wife, Sabina Poppaea, lived here at the *Villa Poppaea* before she married him and was supposedly kicked to death for her pains. The evidence is slightly sketchy, however. What is sure is that this small site has a profusion of excellently preserved Roman wall-paintings, especially in the triclinium (room 14) and the calidarium (room 8) in the south-western corner of the site. There's also a peaceful cloistered area and the whole place retains the comfortable feel of a wealthy out-of-town villa.

! Spartacus, aka Kirk Douglas, the rebel slave, set up his base on
● Mount Vesuvius in 73 AD.

Herculaneum

corso Resina 6, Ercolano, **T** 081-7390963. *Apr-Oct 0830-0730, last entry 1800; Nov-Mar 0830-1700, last entry 1530. €8.50 including same-day visits to Oplontis, Boscoreale and Stabia. €13.50 includes all the former plus Pompeii over a five-day period. Audioguide €5.16. From the station walk straight down the hill for about five minutes to reach the ruins.* See Getting around, p26

Not far from Naples, Herculaneum resembles Naples' Centro Storico strongly in its traditional Roman street layout, with perpendicular streets (Cardo III, IV and V) coming off two main east-west roads: the *Decumanus Inferiore* and *Decumanus Massimo*.

It is a small site in comparison to Pompeii, partly because so much of it remains under an enormous quantity of volcanic rock and mud. This volcanic mud is the secret of Herculaneum's preservation: much more than Pompeii's mixture of ash and pumice, Herculaneum's mud solidified and sealed in the town below, preserving organic substance and the upper storeys of houses.

The scale of the eruption is appreciable when crossing the bridge to the southern edge of the site. Below is what used to be the seafront. The cliff behind gives some kind of idea of the enormous quantity of mud that engulfed the town. Some three hundred or so bodies were found here at the old shoreline in the 1980s: awaiting rescue from the sea, their bodies carbonized by the extreme heat (probably around 400ºC) of Vesuvius's pyroclastic cloud before being buried deep in mud. In the **Casa del bel Cortile** three of these figures are on display, their skeletons still clinging together.

Less gruesomely, many of Herculaneum's buildings and mosaics are in exceptionally good nick. The **Casa di Nettuno e Anfitrite** on Cardo IV has a beautiful mosaic of the eponymous couple, and just to the south the well-preserved women's baths have an excellent mosaic floor. Where the lower Decumanus crosses Cardo V a **Thermopolium**, a shop which sold food, still has intact some ceramic pots set into rectangular counters. Just to the south of this is the town brothel. At the southern edge of town, between Cardo III and Cardo IV, the trunk of a Roman pear tree was found in the garden of the **Casa dell'Albergo**. Pear trees have been planted here again to recreate the orchard that might have once been.

Ercolano

Villa Campolieto, corso Resina, 283, Ercolano, T 081-7322134 www.villevesuviane.net Tue-Sun 1000-1300, free. Details of other villas from Ente per le Ville Vesuviane, at this address.

If you have time to spare in modern-day Ercolano, there are some impressive 18th-century villas with gardens which can be visited. A five-minute walk to the east of the ruins, **Villa Campolieto** is the centre for the *Ente per le Ville Vesuviane*, an organization trying to resurrect many of these crumbling mansions. **Villa Ruggiero** is a little northeast of here. **Villa Favorita**, slightly further east, was closed at the time of writing.

Vesuvius

Buses, cars and taxis go as far as a car park from where the crater is a 20-minute walk up a loose stone path. Entrance to the top of the volcano is €5.16. Buses run from Ercolano station at 1010, 1130 and 1240, returning from Vesuvius at 1240, 1350 and 1500. Tickets, €3.10, are only available from Bar Vesuvio, outside the station. Minibus taxis also do the run from outside the station at €10 per person return, though they will only go when there are enough passengers to make it worth their while.

Towering 1281 metres above the Bay of Naples, and over the lives of everyone who lives there, Vesuvius is far from being the world's biggest or most active volcano, but it's probably its most famous. Around a million people live and work in the *communi vesuviani* on and around its base, within a radius which could be destroyed in the first 15 minutes of a medium to large scale eruption. Hundreds of thousands more would be at least seriously affected by such an eruption. Scientific opinion seems divided only about when, rather than if, Vesuvius will erupt again. A report published in *Science Magazine* in November 2001 found that 8 km under Vesuvius is a 400 sq km reservoir of molten rock, much bigger than previously thought.

Climbing to its summit and peering down into its crater is well worth the effort, though it can be somewhat humbling, and on windy days downright precarious. Souvenir stalls selling postcards and black stone buddhas, skulls, elephants and winged horses add a surreal touch to the experience. (The **Somma Rim**, which forms the distinctive second, lower peak, is the remains of a previous volcano which collapsed some 17,000 years ago.)

When Vesuvius erupted in 79AD it hadn't erupted for about 700 years, the summit was wooded and it seems that the local population were unaware of the mountain's volcanic nature. Pliny the Younger described the eruption in two letters, detailing the column of ash which rose from the volcano in the shape of a pine tree and the pyroclastic flow which killed many of Herculaneum's victims. Explosive volcanic eruptions on the massive scale experienced in 79AD are now referred to by vulcanologists as 'plinian' after Pliny, and it seems that Vesuvius goes through a cycle where a period of dormancy is followed by a plinian or sub-plinian eruption and then a period of smaller eruptions. It may be that the sub-plinian eruption of 1631, which followed a long period of calm, and which killed around 3,500 people, was the beginning of such a cycle. This cycle may have ended with the most recent eruption, in 1944, when 26 people were killed. In total there have been about 35 eruptions since 79AD.

Other than 79AD, six previous plinian eruptions of Somma/Vesuvius have been identified. Of these, those of 5960 and 3580BC are among the biggest-known European volcanic eruptions. Recent digs at Nola, just outside Naples, have uncovered Bronze Age settlements buried by an eruption of the volcano around 2000BC. Finds include intact huts, vases and headgear decorated with a boar's tusks.

West to the Campi Flegrei

West of Naples' ugly suburbs, steaming volcanic landscapes and the remains of some of the earliest Greek and Roman settlements exist side-by-side and often of top of each other.

*****Pozzuoli*** *is a pleasant enough place, without ever being exactly picturesque. Where once was Italy's most important port now there are some distinctive yellow ferries which do the short trip to Ischia via Procida and a few fishing boats. It does, however, have some impressive Roman remains including* ***Anfiteatro Flavio***, *Italy's third-biggest amphitheatre, and in* ***Solfatara***, *one of the area's strangest, smelliest and most striking places. There are several churches too, one of which, the* ***Santuario di San Gennaro***, *just to the south of Solfatara, marks the spot where Naples' patron saint was beheaded.*

Once full of holiday villas of the Roman nobility, modern ***Baia*** *has little sense of its one-time opulence. Indeed much of ancient Baia is now under water. However, a wander around its* ***Parco Archeologico*** *quickly shows why this was once such a desirable spot. These terraces look down over the bay below and the whole complex still has an atmosphere of peaceful grandeur despite its dilapidation.*

Whereas the other ancient remains in the area are most definitely Roman, ***Cuma's Acropoli*** *predate the Roman Empire. Though there is little to be seen of the original Greek temples, the Romans having updated the structures, the* ***Cave of the Sibyl*** *is remarkably intact and the feel of the place is quite un-Roman. It is magical: high above the sea, surrounded by oak trees, a paved path winds up to the* ***Tempio di Giove*** *at the top of the hill. The ruins here are very much ruins, but are no less atmospheric for that.*

▸▸ *See p25 for information on getting to the following sights*

!
The volcanic area around Pozzuoli suffers from an effect known as 'Bradeyism' where the earth's crust rises or falls large amounts over time. Evidence of this can be seen at the Tempio di Serapide (see p90) where the columns bear the marks of molluscs from a time when they were underwater.

◉ Sights

'Tempio di Serapide'
via Serapide, Pozzuoli. *The complex is sunk down in the middle of a piazza just behind the port, to the right as you come out of the Cumana station.*

The so-called Temple of Serapis in the centre of Pozzuoli in fact turns out not to be a temple at all, but rather a humble market from the first or second centuries AD. It's still more often than not referred to as the Tempio though. As markets go it's a pretty grand affair, complete with marble columns, rooms and open spaces. (The two larger rooms behind the four big columns were apparently public toilets.)

Anfiteatro Flavio
via Terracciano 75, **T** 081-5266007. *0900-1hr before sunset. €4, valid for two days including entrance to the remains at Baia and Cuma. Walk uphill for about five minutes from behind tourist information in Pozzuoli to reach the amphitheatre or take bus 152 or P9.*

Italy's third biggest amphitheatre, which, once upon a time, would have seated around 20,000 spectators, is, on the surface, rather dilapidated, not unlike the modern urban jungle that now surrounds it. Underneath, however, everything is extraordinarily well-preserved. An enormous and slightly creepy maze of tunnels, caverns and arches is littered with sizable chunks of old columns. This is where the wild animals were kept while waiting to feast on Christian martyrs. Perhaps most amazing of all, however, are the fragments of Roman statues and carved stone piled up around the outside edge of the amphitheatre. Look carefully here and you will find a Roman foot, the grass growing up around it.

Vulcano Solfatara
via Solfatara 161, Pozzuoli, **T** 081-5262341, www.solfatara.it
0830-1 hr before sunset. €4.60.

Another mile further up the hill above the centre of Pozzuoli the enormous crater of Solfatara, 770 m across at its widest point, is still bubbling and hissing away, though its last eruption is thought to have been in 1198. This weird alien landscape of white sulphurous sand is punctuated by various fumaroles, where steam comes out of the ground at around 160°C. In the centre a pool of mud boils vigorously. The smells vary from that of spent matches to very rotten eggs and there is a constant sound of hissing, bubbling and boiling. The most active parts are fenced off, though you can get pretty close, and the ground all around steams. It's not entirely surprising that the Romans saw it as one of the entrances to hell.

★ Cuma
via Montecuma **T** 081-8543060. *Tue-Sun 0900-1 hr before sunset. €4 valid for two days including entrance to the remains at Baia and Pozzuoli. The remains are actually a couple of km from the Circumflegrea station of Cuma. Easiest access is by bus from Baia (every hour at about half past the hour from in front of the station on the opposite side of the road) or from outside Fusaro station (every half hour).*

Cuma was probably the earliest Greek settlement in Western Europe, and in Greek legend the **Temple of Apollo** was where Daedalus landed, having lost his son Icarus en route from Knossos.

The highlight is definitely the **Cave of the Sibyl**, however. This extraordinary 130-m trapezoidal gallery carved out of the rock may have originally had a military or funerary use, but its sacred feel makes it seem much better suited to its mystical role as home of the reader of oracles. This is (at least according to Virgil) where Aeneas received instructions to descend to the

★ **Cave of the Sibyl, Cuma**
The haunting hollowed-out space of the Sibyl's cave has uncertain ori-
gins, probably predating the ancient Greek settlement.

underworld, and where Tarquin received the Sibylline books which dictated the destiny of Rome. At the end of a winding path at the top of the hill the **Temple of Jupiter** is another awe-inspiring spot with enormous chunks of stone, remnants of pillars and views down over the coast below.

Museo Archeologico dei Campi Flegrei

Castello di Baia, Bacoli, **T/F** 081-5233797, sanc@interbusiness.it
Tue-Sat 0900-1700, Sun 0900-1900. €4 valid for two days including entrance to remains at Baia, Cuma and Pozzuoli.

At the western end of Baia, high above the town, the imposing Aragonese castle (built 1495) contains the Campi Flegrei Archaeological Museum. The highlight among many finds from the area is probably a recreation of the submerged Nympheum, complete with statues which have been recovered from the sea. Various statues, decorated pillars, coins, jewellery and ceramics make up most of the rest of the collection. There is also a very impressive stone bull's head, a salvaged mosaic floor and a three-dimensional model of the entire area in Roman times, clearly showing its volcanic origins.

Parco Archeologico

via Fusaro 75, Baia, **T** 081-5233797. *Tue-Sun 0900-1 hr before sunset. €4 valid for two days including entrance to the museum and to remains at Cuma and Pozzuoli.*

Steps climb up from in front of Baia station to a park often referred to as the Terme di Baia, though actually the ruins are those of an imperial palace, residence of Roman Emperors from Augustus to Septimus Severus (1st century BC to 3rd century AD). Aside from some fragments of mosaic, little decoration survives. The weirdly echoing and water-filled **Tempio di Mercurio** (actually a part of the baths system) is very well-preserved though, and has the world's oldest large-scale dome, predating that of the Pantheon in Rome.

East to the Sorrento Peninsula

Perched on a plateau above the sea, Sorrento is a seaside town strangely detached from the sea. It's there, but it's a long way down, or perhaps more pertinently, a long way back up afterwards. In a day here you're likely to hear as many English voices as you would in a month in Naples. The Grand Tourists of the 19th century gradually retreated from Naples to this more genteel base and two centuries later they're still here in their busloads. It remains a very civilized place but coming from Naples it can seem a little tame – a pallid version of its big neighbour. It is however, much more at ease with tourism and with itself in general.

It's a relaxed and laid-back town, however, and a good base from which to explore the surrounding hills and coast, some of which is spectacular. The mountainous Sorrento Peninsula has an excellent network of paths running between its many villages and has some good walks, with spectacular views over the Bay of Naples, across to Capri and along the Amalfi Coast.

▸▸ *See Sleeping p136 and Eating and drinking p163*

Sights

Sorrento

(Museo Correale di Terranova: via Correale 50, Sorrento, **T** 081-8781846. *0900-1400, closed Tue.* €5. Giardini di Limoni: *entrance either from via Capasso or Corso Italia. Open 1000-1630.*)

The old centre of town is set back between Marina Piccola and Marina Grande, to the west of the main square, piazza Tasso and the railway station.

Piazza Tasso is the site of a statue of Sorrento's treasured 16th-century poet Torquato Tasso, a vertiginous view down towards Marina Piccola, and cafés vying for space with the traffic.

This is the heart of *passeggiata* (evening stroll) territory, and the passeggiata is a serious affair here.

Further west, to the north of corso Italia, a network of little streets weaves to the edge of the cliffs. Sorrento gets interesting amongst these alleyways, piazzas, shops and churches. One of them, **San Francesco**, near the cliffs, has a beautiful little 14th-century cloister, with flowers tumbling down amongst its gnarled stone columns. Beyond, the **Villa Comunale**, a narrow, shady, tree-lined park, has excellent views across the sea to Capri. A path winds down from here to the marina and cramped beaches far below.

On the corner of via P R Giuliani and via S Cesareo, another of Sorrento's landmarks, the **Sedile Dominova**, is a large open-domed structure complete with 15th-century frescoes. It was once a meeting place for the local aristocracy. Nowadays a working men's club uses it, and card games carry on seemingly oblivious of the staring tourists.

On the south side of corso Italia, the **Catedrale di Sorrento** (originally Romanesque but rebuilt in the 15th century) is strangely dark and gloomy despite its pastel colouring. There are some good examples of local *intarsia* (inlaid wood) work.

● *A little further west along corso Italia is* Bougainvillea, *one of the world's great gelaterie. See also p164.*

Northeast of piazza Tasso (follow via Correale around to its end) the **Museo Correale di Terranova** has a collection of local art and archaeological finds, including some interesting depictions of the town before the onslaught of 20th-century tourism. An over-flowing garden leads down to the cliff edge.

Around the corner from here is a lemon tree plantation, the **Giardini di Limoni**, unexpectedly near the middle of town. It's open to the public and free, presumably in the hope that you will buy some lemon-based products afterwards.

Many of the town's small **beaches** are private though good alternatives can be found around the peninsula (see below).

Penisola Sorrentina

A good map of walking paths is available from tourist information (see p32) in Sorrento or Massa.

Away from Sorrento itself, the rest of the peninsula is a flowery hilly patchwork of lemon and olive groves and quiet towns and villages. Little is wild, the emphasis generally being on manicured cultivation, though the very tip at **Punta Campanello** is an exception to this rule. An excellent network of paths, many of them old mule tracks between terraces of olives and lemons, means that walking is the best way to see the area.

Near Sorrento, a great day can be had doing the route from **Massa Lubrense to Termini and on to Sant'Agata** and back to Sorrento. (A *SITA* bus goes between Sorrento and Sant'Agata via Massa at least once an hour through the day if you wish to shorten this.) High on the ridge of the peninsula above Termini is an excellent place for a picnic, with spectacular views over Capri and the sea to either side.

Near Nerano there are some good beaches: **Marina del Cantone** to the southeast has a good pebbly stretch while a path to the southwest leads to **Capitiello** beach on the steep-sided Baia di Jeranto. Other possibilities are accessible on foot, such as **le Fontane**, due west of Termini, whereas some, such as **Cenito** just to the south, are only reachable from the sea. Boats can be hired from Marina del Cantone or from Sorrento.

The islands

Rising steeply from the sea at either end of the Bay of Naples, Ischia and Procida to the north and Capri to the south must have all once seemed wild, even forbidding places with their steep cliffs dropping down to occasional narrow beaches. Now, however, all three are tamed, cultivated and quite densely populated, entirely at ease with their tourist destination status.

Capri

Somehow managing to retain an atmosphere of chic insouciance even in the face of a tourist onslaught, Capri has remained a playground for the privileged for the last two hundred years, just as it was in Roman times. Capri Town's tiny piazzetta, filled with nonchalant waiters, the well-dressed and expensive cafés, embodies this attitude and is the focus for Caprese strutting and people-watching. Irrespective of sexuality there is something camp about the place too, and the island continues to be a magnet for upwardly mobile young gay men.

*Until a road was carved out of the massive limestone cliff dividing the higher, quieter, **Anacapri** from Capri itself in 1874, the two halves of this island were very much separate, the only connection being the 800 or so steps of the **Scala Fenicia**. Nowadays the island's two parts are united in the pursuit of tourism and it can get unpleasantly packed with visitors in the summer months, especially around the centre of Capri Town, and at some of the more popular sights such as the **Grotta Azzurra**, Tiberius's **Villa Jovis** (from where he ruled the Roman Empire from 27 to 37AD) and the **Villa San Michele**, the 19th-century home of Swedish author Axel Munthe. There are plenty of other caves and old palaces to share around, however, among them the Roman **Villa di Damecuta** and the **Grotta di Matermania**, complete with more Roman remains. And **Marina Piccola**, on the southern edge of the island, has some of the best beaches.*

*Total escape from anything resembling a tourist trap is still possible, however. The most beautiful spot of all on the island is the summit and surroundin74g wild area of **Monte Solaro**, with its views all around, as well as 589 metres almost straight down, and orchids among the 800 different species of wild flowers on its slopes.*

▸▸ *See Sleeping p137 and Eating and drinking p164*

◉ Sights

Grotta Azzurra

A constant flow of boats leaves Marina Grande throughout the day to take you to the grotto (€6 return) but you have to change into a rowing boat in order to enter the cave (another €4.10 plus €4 entrance fee). The first part of the journey can also be done overland, either on foot, or by bus from Anacapri.

Capri's most popular attraction is a cave at the northwest of the island where sunlight beating down from outside shines up through the water inside, creating a distinctly magical blue glow. Just how magic it feels may depend on how many other people are there trying simultaneously to experience the same effect. The best times to go are early in the morning or while everyone else is having lunch. Very early and very late, before and after the rush of boats, it's theoretically possible to swim around into the cave.

Marina Grande

*To avoid the crowds on the funicular (€1.30 single, every 15 minutes, **T** 081-8370420) and the bus (€1.30 single, every 5 or 10 minutes, **T** 081-8370420) take the signposted winding path which goes up the hill from behind the piazza to the eastern end of the seafront. Both the funicular and the buses run from the western end of the port.*

Down the steep hill from Capri Town, the received wisdom about Capri's main port is that it's best to get in and out of it as soon as possible. It's actually not such a bad place, though if you arrive with a thousand or so other people off the ferry all at the same time as you, you may disagree.

Capri Town and around

Parco Astarita open May-Sep 1000-1800, Oct-Apr 1000-1400.

The heart of the island is the town of Capri itself, and the heart of the town is **la Piazzetta**, a tiny piazza squeezed full of chairs from its four expensive cafés. Despite the fact that it can get overrun at busy times it is still a picturesque spot, and an excellent one for a stint of people-watching. Between the piazzetta and the funicular station is an attractive terrace with benches overlooking Marina Grande below.

The one side of the Piazzetta not taken up by cafés is occupied by the **Chiesa di Santo Stefano**, with its distinctive grey and white dome and roof.

To the right of the church via Maria Serafina, one of Capri's most attractive and peaceful streets, winds its way under whitewashed arches before turning into via Castello and climbing to Belvedere Cannone, with great views south over Marina Piccola (where there is a small beach, see below) and the rocky islands of the **Faraglioni**, often used as the symbol of the island.

Another excellent stroll from the piazzetta heads out along the shop-lined via Vittorio Emanuele, via Camerelle and via Tragara to the Belvedere di Tragara, near the Faraglioni, before curving around the southeast corner of the island. A well-built path cuts through a wilder part of the island which passes the Villa Malaparte below, a strange-looking terracotta coloured modernist building constructed in the early 1940s and used as the setting for Jean-Luc Godard's 1963 film *Le Mépris* (Contempt), starring Brigitte Bardot. Just before the path turns inland again, the **Grotta di Matermania** may have been the centre of the cult of the Goddess Cybele, banned by Rome. The remains of two rooms still exist in the cave, with some very faint traces of Roman frescoes. In Roman times it was lined with a barrel-vaulted ceiling, most of which has since collapsed. Beyond the cave up some steep steps at Bar Trattoria *Le Grotelle* (where you may need a drink to recover from the climb up) a short path to the right leads to the **Arco Naturale**: an enormous stone arch towering over the sea below. Via Matermina continues back to the piazzetta.

Heading east out of the piazzetta along via Le Botteghe takes you to the simple and attractive little **Chiesa di San Michele della Croce**. From here via Tiberio heads northeast to Tiberius's villa at the eastern tip of the island. Just before the villa itself, Parco Astarita has three terraces amongst the trees with increasingly impressive views down to the sea and right to the Faraglioni.

Marina Piccola
Giardini Augusto: *0900-1900 daily.*

A handful of somewhat cramped white pebbly beaches sit in between cafés and restaurants here while cliffs tower behind to the west. There are various private beaches which you can pay to access but the public section in the middle is perfectly good and the swimming is excellent, especially through a low natural arch in the rock where there are also some good diving spots.

To the east via Krupp winds along the coast and up a gently climbing switchback path to the flowery **Giardini Augusto** at the southern edge of Capri Town. Officially it's closed due to dangers of rockfalls but locals and rebellious tourists climb past the barriers without seeming particularly concerned.

Villa Jovis
Mon-Sun 0900-1hr before sunset. €2.

Suetonius's *The Twelve Caesars* paints a portrait of Tiberius as a perverted, paranoid and violent Emperor. How much his account is an exaggeration is still hotly debated but the reputation has stuck. Whether Tiberius actually did push people he didn't like much over the edge of the 330-metre Salto di Tiberio is also open to question, but what is more sure is that this is where he ruled the Empire from 27 to 37AD. The four enormous reservoirs around which the complex is built could have contained 8,000 square metres of water, and these and a baths complex survive. Largely, however, the position and the views are more impressive than the ruins themselves.

Anacapri

Buses (€1.30) run from Marina Grande and from the bus station in via Roma in Capri to piazza Vittoria in Anacapri every 10 minutes or so throughout the day.

It is said that until the mid-18th century Capresi would live entire lives on one half of the island without visiting the other. The road, built in 1874, changed that but Anacapri remains slightly more down-to-earth than its self-consciously chic neighbour. The physical differences between the two island halves are best appreciated from the peak of Monte Solaro, or better still, by climbing down the dangerously steep path through il Passetiello. When author Axel Munthe came to the island in the 1920s he chose the Villa San Michele as its most perfect spot and if you can fight through the modern-day pilgrims you might see why. There are other interesting features, such as the elaborate floor of the Chiesa Monumentale San Michele, but generally it is the simple attraction of relative peace and calm that people come here looking for.

The wonderfully colourful majolica tiled floor of the baroque church of **Chiesa Monumentale San Michele** (*0930-1800, €1*) in Anacapri's piazza San Nicola dates from 1761 and features a depiction of paradise complete with cats and dogs, a unicorn, an armadillo and a very yellow Adam and Eve.

Made famous by Axel Munthe's book, the house and gardens of **Villa San Michele** (*viale A Munthe, Anacapri T 081-8371401*

F 081-8373530. Nov-Jan 1030-1530, Mar 0930-1630, Apr, Oct 0930-1700, May-Sep 0930-1800; €5) that he built are kept as they were when he lived here and make it easy to see why the Swedish author fell in love with the place, though these days everything is very well nailed down. *The Story of San Michele*, a forerunner of many later foreigner-living-in-southern-Europe travel books, was published in London in 1929, and has been translated into more than 30 languages.

Fans of the book can see the original typescript in a glass case while everyone else wanders around the covered walkways of the terraced gardens listening to birdsong, peering at Munthe's various pieces of antiquity and admiring the views. At the far tip of the garden a stone sphinx looks over a particularly fine panorama towards the Sorrento Peninsula.

★ Monte Solaro

Halfway between piazza Vittoria and Villa San Michele, via Montesolaro (also signposted "sentiero per Cetrella") heads right up away from the hordes below into a different kind of Capri altogether. The stony path climbs gently through a landscape that becomes progressively less cultivated the higher you go. The real change comes, however, when you get up onto the ridge and a wild valley opens up in front of you. From here you can go left out to **Monte Capello** and beyond through asphodels and orchids in spring, or head right up to the **summit** of Monte Solaro or continue to the beautifully situated monastery at **Cetrella**. If you have time, all three are worth the effort. At the top of Monte Solaro there are some jaw-dropping views, 360 degrees around, and, to the south, 589 vertiginous metres down to Ventroso and the sea below. From Anacapri to the summit takes about 45 minutes, though you'll almost certainly want to stop and admire the view on the way.

Alternatively take the chairlift from the end of via Capodimonte in Anacapri, which is also quite spectacular, and quicker (12 minutes), though less satisfying. €5.50 return, €4 one way.

From the monastery at Cetrella (you can climb the stairs in the church of Santa Maria a Cetrella for yet another view) one of Capri's best-kept secrets, a path down through **il Passetiello**, is a spectacular but precariously steep way down into Capri. It descends what you (and almost everybody else) will have previously considered to be a sheer and impenetrable rockface. Turn immediately right out of the church (a small sign reads "per il passetiello") and follow the path all the way. It is marked with red splodges but isn't hard to follow. It's overgrown at the top, however, and eroded further down and is only suitable for the sure-footed. Allow about 50 minutes to get from Cetrella right back to the piazzetta in Capri.

Ischia

The island of Ischia, once home, at least in mythology, to Typhon, creator of volcanoes, has had no volcanic activity since 1883. But many of its springs still run warm and there is a thriving spa industry. The biggest island in the bay, and one where tourism arrived later than on Capri, Ischia is nevertheless very much a tourist destination. It's still a very beautiful place, however; trees mask a lot of development, and steep slopes prevent too much encroachment into the centre of the island.

*Ischia also has bigger **beaches** than Capri, a spectacularly situated **castle**, a good (if strenuous) walk up to the 787-m summit of **Monte Epomeo**, some sleepy towns, a botanical garden complete with tea house built by British composer William Walton and his wife (**La Mortella**, on the outskirts of Forio on the west coast, **T** 081-986220, www.ischia.it/mortella), and, in **Sant'Angelo**, on the south of the island, one of the Bay of Naples' most attractive villages. Once separate, **Ischia Porto** and **Ischia Ponte** are now joined and often referred to as 'Ischia'. Two distinct centres still exist, however. **Forio**, on the west coast, has an impressive whitewashed church, Chiesa Madonna del Soccorso, on land protruding out into the sea, **Casamicciola Terme** and **Lacco Ameno**, on the north coast, have beaches and spas.*

▸▸ *See Sleeping p138 and Eating and drinking p165*   103

Getting around   A reasonably efficient bus service runs around the island, most routes starting or finishing at the terminus at Ischia Porto (behind the port). The most useful routes are the CD (circolare destra) and CS (circolare sinistra) which run in either direction around the island, stopping at Casamicciola, Lacco Ameno, Forio, Sant'Angelo, Fontana and Barano. They run every 15 minutes or half an hour depending on the time of day. There is also a service (linea 1) every 15 minutes to Sant'Angelo via Forio. Tickets €0.93 single, €2.74 for a whole day and are available from tabacchi and from the terminus.

Sights

Ischia Porto
Ischia Porto is the main bus terminus – see above.

Arriving by sea, the harbour of Ischia Porto was once a volcanic crater, only connected to the sea in 1854 by King Ferdinand II, and its origins are still clear in its shape. Ferries arrive at the western side of the harbour, hydrofoils towards the east. Along the eastern curve of the harbour **via Porto** is entirely made up of bars and restaurants with good views.

● *Bar di Maoi, just off the southeast corner of the harbour, sells particularly good ice-cream. See p166.*

Follow via Porto inland and around to the left and it connects to via Roma which soon becomes the (mainly pedestrianized) corso Vittoria Colonna. A couple of blocks behind via Roma, to the east of the port, **Spiaggia di San Pietro e della Marina** is a good public beach. The beaches east of here are also popular but you have to pay for the privilege.

Corso Vittoria Colonna leads all the way to Ischia Ponte, past upmarket clothes and ceramics shops, restaurants, houses and the occasional church. Roads to the left lead down to various mainly private beaches. About half way along on the left, opposite the tiny church of **San Girolamo** (also known as Madonna della Pace), the pleasantly shaded public park of **Villa Nenzi Bozzi** is filled with trees and birdsong. The church itself has a mosaic dome.

As the road heads downhill to the sea it runs parallel to **Spiaggia dei Pescatori** (Beach of the Fishermen), a beach which is indeed still used by fishermen as well as sunbathers, and has excellent views of the castle (see below).

Ischia Ponte

If you don't fancy the 20-minute walk, bus 7 shuttles back and forth between the port and Ischia Ponte. Castello Aragonese: *Mar-Nov, Mon-Sun 0930-1 hr before sunset.* €8.

The 'ponte' of the name is more a walkway than a bridge, connecting the mainland with the towering fortified island of the **Castello Aragonese**. The first fortress here was built in 474BC by Syracusan Greeks. Conquered variously by the Romans, the Arabs, the Normans, the Swabians, the Angevins and the English, and attacked by nearly everybody else, from the Goths to the Visigoths and the Vandals, the castle remained a vital place of refuge for the islanders, from volcanic explosions as well as pirates and invaders. At the beginning of the 18th century the castle held nearly 2000 families, as well as a convent, an abbey, 13 churches, and a prince. It was also the place where, in the 15th century, Ferrante d'Avalos married the beautiful poet-princess Vittoria Colonna, who later became a great friend of Michelangelo. Today it is an extraordinary maze of steps and walls, simple sun-bleached churches and vine and olive terraces, with panoramic views on all sides.

It's worth allowing a couple of hours to have a look round. A map and notes in English are provided with your ticket, detailing two itineraries around the castle. Highlights include the pentagonal church of **San Pietro a Pantaniello**, the remains of the **Cathedral of the Assunta** (shelled by the British in 1809 in an attempt to take the island from the French) and the beautiful **Olive Terrace**.

In the disturbingly spooky **Nuns' Cemetery**, the bodies of dead nuns were left sitting on stone chairs, their bodies slowly decomposing, fluids collected in special vases beneath, before finally the dried skeletons were collected in the Ossarium. Living nuns would spend hours in here every day contemplating death, and, presumably, contracting diseases and mental health problems.

There's a lift up and down, though the walk (down, at least) through Alphonse of Aragon's tall 15th-century carved-out tunnel is recommended.

Sant'Angelo
Giardini Termali Aphrodite, www.aphrodite.it Tickets available from tourist information, via Chiaia delle Rose 16, **T** 081-986333. *0900-1900.*

Sleek cats laze in the sun on bleached pastel-coloured walls in traffic-free and picturesque Sant'Angelo in the south of the island. The place retains a more Italian feel than the rest of the island and has a spa and a decent beach immediately to the east (**Spiaggia dei Maronti**), being recreated at the time of writing after having been washed away for the second time in recent years.

The town tumbles down a steep hillside to an isthmus connecting the mainland to an attractive but inaccessible rocky outcrop. There are plenty of cafés and restaurants along the seafront in which to laze the day away, or you could pay for a day or half-day in the **Giardini Termali Aphrodite**: a large complex of 12 pools, hot springs, waterfalls, saunas and beauty centres belonging to the *Park Hotel Miramare* (see p138).

Monte Epomeo
Signposted path from Fontana.

With an almost 360-degree view of the island, and 787 m above the sea, the rocky peak of Monte Epomeo is well worth the steep climb from Fontana. The sun-dappled path passes among chestnut trees before opening out at the top to spectacular views down over abandoned terraces and the coast below. The path to and from Forio is less well signposted but is a good alternative way down.

Procida

*It's not hard to see why Procida is popular as a film set (parts of Il Postino and The Talented Mr Ripley were filmed here). The island has a worn, photogenic appeal: the jumbled sun-bleached and peeling pastel painted houses with their external stairs have an air of authenticity that is often missing on the other islands, and the fishing industry is alive and well. (The downside of all this authenticity being that some of the beaches are fairly liberally scattered with flotsam and jetsam.) Picture postcard Procida is especially prominent at **Marina Grande**, the island's main hub where ferries arrive and depart, and at the fishing port of **Corricella**, a 10-minute walk over the other side of the island, below the imposing bulk of the ex-prison of **Castello d'Avalos** and the walled village and church of **Terra Murata**.*

*The rest of the island to the south, is less picturesque, and quite heavily populated, especially in the centre. As you work your way out to the various peninsulas it becomes slightly more wild, especially at **Punta Pizzaco**, where flat rock is punctuated with broom, succulents and cacti, and paths wind around above the lapping sea. The island's third arrival and departure point at **Marina Chiaiolella** is more geared up for yachts than fishing boats or ferries but is an attractive place, with a couple of decent restaurants. To the west of here is the island's best beach, **Spiaggia Chiaiolella**. The volcanic crescent of **Vivara** is a nature reserve at the southern tip of the island, joined to Procida by a bridge. This has been unsafe for years, however, and until it's finally repaired there is no public access.*

▸▸ *See Sleeping p139 and Eating and drinking p167*

Getting around *The island is small enough to walk around, though especially in the centre the roads can feel less than safe for pedestrians at times. There are places on Marina Grande where you can rent bikes or scooters if you want to get around a bit quicker. There are also taxi ranks next to the tourist information office, just to the west of the ferry terminal, and the ferry ticket offices.*

 Sights

Chiesa Abbaziale di San Michele
via G Marconi 4, **T** 338-4168001, www.abbaziasanmichele.it
0945-1245, 1500-1700. Closed Sun pm. Museum €2.

At the heart of the walled village of Terra Murata, this church has strange and slightly morbid hidden depths. On the site of an 11th-century Benedictine monastery, the highlight of a rather eclectic church interior is a winged, sword-wielding statue of San Michele from 1727. The so-called museum is really a guided tour of the library and various chapels and catacombs underneath the church. There seems to be an increasing obsession with skulls and bones the deeper down you go.

Watersports
See sports p208 for lists of dive operators and boat hire.

Boats are available for rent, from yachts to little motor boats and you can also do diving courses in the waters around the island.

★ Terra Murata
Procida's Terra Murata is less of a fortified castle and more of an eccentrically jumbled collection of buildings on a hill.

Amalfi Coast

One of Europe's most famous stretches of coast, and the backdrop for many a car advert, the Amalfi Coast snakes its way along the southern edge of the Sorrento Peninsula, its villages and towns precariously stuck onto the sides of mountains plummeting into the sea. In fact, coming by car or bus, the road is as much part of the excitement as arriving; sitting on the seaward side is a nail-bitingly gripping a fairground ride.

Positano

In their days as maritime powers, between the ninth and 12th centuries, Positano was Amalfi's poorer neighbour. Now, however, the situation is very much reversed, and the town is the rich kid of the Amalfi Coast. Its hotels have more stars, its restaurants are more expensive, and its boutiques cater to a more upmarket clientele.

Positano's success in offering itself as an exclusive destination is due in no small part to its extraordinary location: more spectacular than Amalfi, its houses (and hotels) stick to the rounded sides of a steep valley and while the coast road rumbles along higher up the hill, little traffic is allowed down into the town, most of which is connected by paths and steps.

*Its lack of conventional 'sights' (the **Chiesa di Santa Maria Assunta** is about the nearest it gets) is made up for by a couple of good **beaches** in **Marina Grande** and **Fornillo**, and some vertiginous **walks** up the mountainsides behind the town. Most people here just wander, however, stopping frequently for breaks in cafés, restaurants and shops. The latter are supposedly famous for their 'fashion', though much of this seems slightly stuck in a time-warp from the days when Positano fashion actually was fashionable, during the 1950s and 1960s. The town claims to have been the first to import the bikini into Italy.*

▶▶ *See Sleeping p140 and Eating and drinking p168*

Getting there Buses leave from opposite the station in Sorrento (also stopping at Meta which is quicker coming from Naples) every half an hour or so (€1.19). Ferries go to and from: Capri (1 a day, €10, **T** 089-811164); Salerno and Amalfi (5 a day, €5/€4, **T** 089-873190); and in July and August, Naples (3 a day, **T** 089-811986). Booths down by the ferry pier offer boat trips to the Grotta Smeralda (Emerald Grotto), Isole Li Galli and Nerano as well as night excursions and private boat hire: Lucibello, via del Brigantino 9, **T** 089-875032, www.lucibello.it

◉ Sights

Chiesa Nuova
Buses from Sorrento or Amalfi stop at the western end of the top of the town, by Bar Internazionale. *Just behind here up the narrow via Chiesa Nuova, is the church. It's often closed, however.*

The floor of the church dates from the 1600s and is probably from the Neapolitan Chiajese School, which was also responsible for the tiles in the Santa Chiara Cloister in Naples.

Marina Grande and Fornillo
Santa Maria Assunta: *Mon-Sun 0700-2000.*

Viale Pasitea and a series of steps lead from the bus stop to Santa Maria Assunta and Marina Grande. At the western end of the beach ferries arrive and depart, but it's more of a beach than a port.

Behind the ferry pier a path leads around the cliff to Fornillo beach, a quieter version of Marina Grande, and good for swimming.

Behind the Marina Grande to the eastern end, the **Chiesa di Santa Maria Assunta** has a colourfully tiled dome, though the interior is less impressive. The highlight is a 13th-century Byzantine Madonna and Child on the high altar, more gold leaf than not.

Sentiero Santa Maria del Castello
Allow a good hour for the ascent, 40 minutes or so for the descent.

This path heading up the mountain behind Positano starts from behind the Chiesa Nuova. From via Chiesa Nuova continue past the church up steps which soon reach a road. Cross this and follow the steps up on the other side. This soon becomes a steep path which switchbacks all the way up to Santa Maria del Castello, over 650 m above sea level. In spring there seems to be a different species of flower on every bend, and the views, unsurprisingly, are excellent.

Amalfi and Atrani

There is little in its popularity as a contemporary holiday destination and its picturesque setting to suggest that Amalfi was ever much more than a pleasant fishing town with some nice old churches and buildings. In fact, between the 9th and 12th centuries, it was an independent republic with a population of up to 80,000, and one of the foremost maritime powers of the Mediterranean, on a par with Genoa, Pisa and Venice.

*There are some good walks to be had inland up the verdant **Valle dei Mulini** (Valley of the Mills), or up steep steps under cliffs and through lemon groves to **Pontone**. Alternatively you can just laze on the **beach**: Amalfi has eight 'private beach establishments' which you pay for the privilege of using. The free public section in the middle of town (near the Flavio Gioia monument) is perfectly acceptable, however. From the area around Lido Azzurro at the western end of Amalfi there are several places where you can rent boats or book trips to the **Grotta Smeralda** (Emerald Grotto). **Atrani** is Amalfi's smaller and quieter Siamese sibling, a jumble of narrow whitewashed alleys squashed onto the coast to the east and a good, easy escape from the crowds.*

▸▸ *See Sleeping p141 and Eating and drinking p168*

◉ Sights

Duomo and Museum

Museum: 1000-1700 winter, 0900-2100 summer. €2.50. During these times access to cathedral through museum only. Cathedral also open from 0730.

Amalfi's 13th-century Duomo is at the centre of the town up an imposing set of steps. The brass doors, imported from Constantinople, were cast around the middle of the 11th century and may be Italy's oldest. The interior has been recently restored to its pre-Baroque state, though it is disappointingly lacking in atmosphere after its striking black and white exterior and handsome campanile. More impressive is the **Chiostro del Paradiso**, a Moorish jungle of columns and arches around a small garden. The **museum** contains a 13th-century statue of Saint Elias looking distinctly wizard-like, a grand 17th-century silver crosier and a bejewelled Angevin mitre embedded with 19,000 pearls. There are also temporary art exhibitions held here. Under the cathedral, the **Crypt of St Andrew** contains the remains of the apostle, looted from Constantinople during the Crusades in 1206.

Museo della Carta

via delle Cartiere 23, **T** 089-8304561, www.museodellacarta.it
Mar-Oct Mon-Sun 1000-1800; Nov-Feb Mon-Sun 1000-1300, €3.40.

With its early trade connections with the Orient, in the 12th century Amalfi was one of the first places in Europe to bring back the technology of paper-making, and its handmade paper was much sought after for centuries. Handmade paper is still made in the town, using the impressive 18th-century water-powered production methods you can see on display here, in a mill dating from the 13th or 14th century.

With the ticket into the museum you get a guided tour (in English and Italian) of the machinery and tools that were used. The quality of the tour depends very much on the guide, but they can be fascinating.

Museo Civico
piazza del Municipio 6. *Mon-Fri 0800-1400, Tue and Thu 1600-1900. Closed Sat and Sun. Free.*

The so-called Museo Civico is really nothing more than the town hall, but it does contain an original copy of the **Tavole Amalfitane**, a set of maritime laws in force from medieval times until the 16th century. Also here are some other manuscripts, paintings and the costumes of the Historical Court of Amalfi which are worn every year by the participants in the Palio delle Quattro Repubbliche Marinare, a ceremonial boat race between Amalfi, Genoa, Pisa and Venice (see festivals, p190).

Atrani
About a 20-minute walk from eastern end of Amalfi (see below).

More residential than its better-known neighbour, Atrani is a fascinating maze of stepped paths, dark passageways and houses piled higgledy-piggledy on top of each other. It has a pretty, café-filled central piazza and can be a merciful escape from Amalfi's crowds.

From the eastern end of Amalfi, steps (the **Salita Roberto Guiscardo**) head up from the main road and become a winding path parallel with the road below. This leads through covered

!
• Full bottles of water on steps and windowsills of houses in Atrani are, depending on who you listen to, either to ward off evil spirits or to dissuade cats from peeing there. There seems to have been little serious study of its efficacy for either.

passageways, between peeling whitewashed houses and along a sunny stretch with good views all the way to piazza Umberto I in Atrani, about 20 minutes walk away.

Ravello

*This town of mainly traffic-free lanes, villas and gardens, high walls and panoramic views down to the coast below has a superior air and has long been a destination for the rich and famous. Its quiet streets have played host to all manner of élite personages: the Bloomsbury group stayed in the **Villa Cimbrone**, DH Lawrence wrote part of Lady Chatterley's Lover here and Graham Greene some of The Third Man, Greta Garbo eloped here, Vittorio Emanuele III abdicated and Wagner, Liszt, John F Kennedy and EM Forster all put in appearances too. Various plaques around the place commemorate the visitors.*

*The handsome **Duomo** looks down over the attractive piazza Duomo. Off to the south of this the **Villa Rufolo** has great views from its gardens. The best way to see the grand Villa Cimbrone is to stay in its hotel, but you can also visit the gardens with the rest of the plebs during the day. Off via San Giovanni del Toro the **Belvedere Principessa di Piemonte** affords great views of the coast to the east. The walk from Ravello down to Amalfi via Atrani (allow about an hour and a half) is strongly recommended: paths and steep steps go down between lemon groves with great views of the coast below.*

Sights

Il Duomo
piazza del Duomo, Ravello. **T** 089-858311. *Mon-Sun 9.30-1300, 1500-1900. Museum €1.50.*

The highlight of Ravello's 11th-century cathedral is probably its finely cast old brass doors designed by Barisano da Trani in 1179.

You have to go inside to see them. There is also a Giotto-esque Madonna and Child and a couple of fine pulpits from the 12th and 13th centuries, one supported by stone lions, the other decorated with mosaics of Jonah being eaten and regurgitated. The **museum** downstairs contains some of the items removed when the church was restored in the 1980s and a beautiful 13th-century marble bust of Sichelgaita Rufolo of the famous local family.

★ Villa Rufolo, Ravello
One of the Amalfi Coast's most photographed views, the backdrop of the gardens of the Villa Rufolo is also a feature of the renowned outdoor summer concerts.

★ Villa Rufolo

piazza del Duomo, **T** 089-857096. *Mon-Sun 0900-30 mins before sunset, or earlier in case of concerts.* €4.
Concerts: **T** 089-858149, **F** 089-858249, www.ravelloarts.org €20.

Originally the villa of a family of rich merchants who are mentioned in Boccaccio's *Decameron*, this grand 13th-century villa was a ruin until it was purchased and sympathetically restored by a Scot, Francis Reid, in the middle of the 19th century. The romantic atmosphere has been retained, and not too much rebuilt. The gardens overflow with flowers and the views are spectacular. Classical music concerts take place here through the year, in the summer outside in the gardens. Some of these are excellent. You can book online in advance.

Villa Cimbrone

via Santa Chiara 26, **T** 089-857459. *Mon-Sun 0900 to 30 mins before sunset.* €4.

Constructed at the beginning of the 20th century, Villa Cimbrone has none of the authenticity of Villa Rufolo, though that's not to say that it's not very beautiful. Designed by an Englishman, Lord Grimthorpe, also responsible for Big Ben, the villa itself is a five-star hotel complete with helipad but the gardens can be visited by all. The highlight is the **Terrazzo dell'Infinito**, Terrace of the Infinite, where classical busts dot the enormous coastal view.

Further afield

Away from the Bay and the Amalfi Coast, Campania has plenty more to offer which is still within striking distance. Two places stand out, however, as excellent day trips: Caserta and Paestum. The former has the Reggia di Caserta, an enormous palace often called 'the Versailles of the South' but quite grand enough to not need such comparisons. To the south of Salerno, Paestum, for centuries forgotten in dense malarial jungle, is possibly the world's best-preserved ancient Greek site. Three majestic temples rise above the Paestum Plain, and around them the remains of a Greek, and subsequently Roman, city.

Paestum

Of all the extraordinary sites around Naples, Paestum is both the most awesome and the most romantic. In a peaceful setting on plains to the south of Salerno, with mountains rising up in the distance, three enormous Greek temples stand in a rural landscape surrounded by the ruins of their city, the bulk of their structures still extraordinarily intact two and a half thousand years after they were built. The number of flowers and lizards is far greater than the number of tour groups, and parts of the site are overgrown with trees, bushes, wild flowers and herbs. Among these may be the wild descendants of the roses for which the Greek city was once famous.

★ Paestum site
Mon-Sun 0900-1hr before sunset, last entry 1hr prior to that. €4, or combined museum/site ticket €6.50. Museum: Mon-Sun 0845-1900, last entry 1830, closed 1st and 3rd Monday of each month. €4, or combined museum/site ticket €6.50. It's a pleasant 10-minute walk from the station, through a gate in the old city walls and down a long straight road to the site. See also p26. There are also buses which leave from the piazza Concordio in Salerno.

History

Poseidonia was founded by Greeks from nearby Sybaris around 600BC. Well-defended by its 3 miles of city walls (still standing, and of their time probably the best-preserved in the world), near important trade routes, and surrounded by a fertile plain, it grew wealthy and became one of the most important Greek centres in Magna Grecia. The Romans took over after 273BC and renamed it Paestum, constructing new buildings such as the baths, the amphitheatre and the Temple of Peace. Thereafter the city slowly fell into decline. Deforestation in the mountains dangerously altered the courses of local rivers, trade routes moved further north and the surrounding area became an increasingly malarial swamp and was subject to Saracen raids. In medieval times local villagers used the Temple of Athena as a Christian church, but until the middle of the 18th century the city was largely overgrown and forgotten. When in 1752 a road was built between Salerno and Agropoli, engineers stumbled upon the city while hacking their way through the forest. They continued nevertheless, their road cutting straight through the amphitheatre, an act for which they were later prosecuted.

Coming from the station, turning right at the end of the road from the Porta Sirena takes you along past the amphitheatre on the left and the museum on the right to the entrance by the elegant **Temple of Athena** (also known erroneously as the Temple of Ceres), built around 500BC, and with both Doric and Ionic elements. Terracotta ex-voto statues of Athena were found here, and many can be seen in the museum (see below).

At the southern end of the site stand two even larger Doric temples, probably both dedicated to Hera, though they are usually known as the **Basilica** and the **Temple of Neptune**. The Basilica is the oldest (circa 550BC) and the largest, with 50 tapering outer columns with slight convex curves. This method, known as entasis, accentuates the weight of the upper structure and produces the illusion of straight lines from a distance.

The so-called **Temple of Neptune**, built around 450BC, is the best-preserved of the three, still with gables at either end. Some suggest that this temple may have been dedicated to Apollo.

In comparison to the temples, the **rest of the Greek and Roman town** is much more ruined, though the small amphitheatre, the forum, swimming baths and various other buildings and paved roads all survive in one form or another.

The **Museo Nazionale di Paestum** has some very fine Greek pieces from in and around the city, including terracotta statues, bronze pots (some of which were sealed with wax and still contained soft honey when they were found), perfume bottles, and various pieces of ceramics and stone carvings. There is also a room upstairs of Roman finds. Pride of place, however, goes to the unique tomb paintings, and especially the Tomb of the Diver. These frescoes are almost the only surviving examples of Greek painting, and the image on the inside of the lid of the Tomb of the Diver in particular has become a symbol of the whole civilization. Found a mile south of the city and containing remnants of a lyre, it is thought to be the tomb of a musician. The image of the diver itself represents death and the leaving of the borders of the inhabited world and of human knowledge to enter the ocean: the unknown but also the source of all other forms of knowledge.

Caserta

Caserta, about 12 miles north of Naples, was an entirely unremarkable town until King Charles III of Bourbon decided in 1750 that it was the perfect place, away from volcanoes and invading Saracens, to build a grand royal palace (reggia) to rival those of Versailles in France and Schönbrunn in Austria. Though a pleasant town, the palace and its grand park still dominate the place, and remain Caserta's only real attractions.

Reggia

*via Douet 2, Caserta, **T** 082-3321400. Park and Gardens: Tue-Sun 0830-1hr before sunset, last entry 2hrs before sunset. Closed Mon. Royal Apartments: Tue-Sun 0830-1930, last entry 1900. Closed Mon. Combined ticket €6. There are buses and trains to Caserta from piazza Garibaldi in Naples, see p26. The Reggia is opposite Caserta's station.*

The comparison most often made about the Reggia is to Versailles. In actual fact the Reggia of today is a rather down-at-heel version of its French counterpart, though certainly in terms of scale it is every bit its equal. Designed by Naples' great Baroque architect Luigi Vanvitelli, work was begun in 1752 and continued under Vanvitelli's son Carlo after his father's death in 1773. It was not until the completion of the decoration of the throne room in 1847 that the palace was properly finished. By that point King Charles' original concept of moving the entire administration of the Kingdom of the Two Sicilies to Caserta had been abandoned but the palace was already well-used as a royal summer residence. After Italian unification in 1860 it was used by the military and the air force continue to occupy many of the rooms today.

The building, 252 metres by 202 metres, is constructed around four large courtyards. From the octangular vestibule at the centre of the triple-arched gallery which crosses the palace, the magnificent **Grand Staircase** leads up to the **Royal Apartments** watched over by a pair of marble lions. On the first floor the throne room is perhaps the grandest of all, and the 19th-century royal bedroom and bathroom of Francis II are suitably regal.

Other highlights include the **Court Theatre**, a scaled-down version of the San Carlo opera house in Naples and complete with an enormous crown over the royal box from which drapery hangs.

! The Reggia's Grand Staircase was used as a set for both *Star Wars* Episode One: The Phantom Menace, and *Star Wars* Episode Two: Attack of the Clones.

The park, also designed by Vanvitelli, extends for about 2 km along a series of ponds, fountains and waterfalls with an increasingly impressive view back to the Reggia. If you don't fancy the walk, various forms of transport are available for hire, from taxis to horses and carts to two- or four-seater pedal-powered vehicles.

At the very top of the park, to the right of the fountain of Venus and Adonis as you approach from the Reggia, is the entrance to the **Giardino Inglese**, a slightly ridiculous, but in places very beautiful, mix of fake ruins, ponds and trees, the centrepiece of which is the semicircular **Cryptoportico** and the **Bath of Venus**. The garden was planned by Queen Maria Carolina of Habsburg and begun in 1786.

Sleeping

There was, until recently, a distinct gap in the Neapolitan hotel market between the up-market and the run-down. Now, however, there are some good mid-range hotels around, often in attractive old buildings. Prices are cheaper in Naples than in most of the rest of Italy and there are some veritable bargains to be had. The Centro Storico has some interesting, but well-hidden, hotels, while those in Santa Lucia tend to be more luxurious and swanky. Cheap-but-central options are generally around the noisy corso Umberto I and piazza Garibaldi area and there are also plenty of quieter, but less convenient places further out in Chiaia, Mergellina, Posillipo and Vomero.

Outside the city there is more choice but prices are higher, especially in places like Capri and Positano. You could try renting an apartment or finding a bed and breakfast room (see *Rent a Bed*, opposite). Bear in mind that outside the city (especially on the islands) places may not be open all year round, particularly between November and March and will be busy in the summer so booking is advisable.

€ **Sleeping codes**

Price				
LL	€300 and over	C	€75-100
L	€250-300	D	€50-75
AL	€200-250	E	€35-50
A	€150-200	F	€25-35
B	€100-150	G	€25 and under

Prices of a double room in high season

Rent a Bed, vico Sergente Maggiore 16, Naples. **T/F** 081-417721, www.rentabed.com *Map 3, E3, p250* This useful and efficient service books apartments and bed and breakfasts in private houses in the Naples area. It's especially comprehensive for the city of Naples itself, where some rooms are available in attractive old palazzi, though you often have to share a bathroom. They can also book hotels. Staff speak English and rooms can also be booked from the English-language website. Prices start at €21 per person per night.

Santa Lucia

LL Excelsior, via Partenope 48, **T** 081-7640111, **F** 081-7649743. *Opposite Castel dell'Ovo and near the junction with via Santa Lucia. Map 3, K4, p251* One of the city's most elegant and luxurious hotels, the Excelsior comes complete with chandeliers, Persian rugs and large quantities of marble. Rooms away from the seaward side have been recently refurbished. All the rooms are very generously sized. Those facing the sea retain a more antique feel and the balconies have superb views, but, like all hotels along this stretch, are far from quiet. The restaurant is on an attractive roof terrace.

LL Santa Lucia, via Partenope 46, **T** 081-7640666 **F** 081-7648580. *Opposite Castel dell'Ovo and the other side of the junction with via Santa Lucia from Excelsior. Map 3, K4, p251* This five-star Grand Hotel is indeed very grand, with excellent views from its Liberty-style rooms of the Bay, the Castel dell'Ovo and borgo Marinaro, the restaurant-filled marina it faces. Its staff are, of course, impeccably attentive and its Partenope Suite is spectacular. Paintings, statues and mirrors abound and there's a roof-garden pool.

A Miramare, via N Sauro 24, **T** 081-7647589, **F** 081-7640775. *Map 3, I5, p251* The 1914 art nouveau-style Miramare is a charming alternative to its more expensive neighbours. The roof terrace has beautiful views and is an excellent spot for the buffet breakfast. The rooms are elegantly decorated and have balconies and generous bathrooms. Even the lift is eminently stylish.

B Rex, via Palepoli 12, **T** 081-7649389, **F** 081-7649227, www.hotel-rex.it *Off via Gen. G Orsini. Map 3, J4, p251* Slightly back from the seafront, Rex is nevertheless a very pleasant hotel in an excellent position. Service is affable and efficient and the décor is sober but reasonably stylish. Rooms have balconies, a/c and some bathrooms are large and have actual baths.

B Chiaja Hotel de Charme, via Chiaia 216 (1st floor), **T** 081-415555, **F** 081-422344, www.hotelchiaia.it *On the right, a short walk up from piazza del Plebiscito. Map 3, F2, p251* Selling themselves on the fact that this was the villa of Marquis Nicola Lecaldano Sasso III, this is certainly a hotel of some style, fitted out with antique furnishings and with excellent service. What it lacks in views it makes up for in creature comforts, from satellite TV to jacuzzis and it's about as central as it is possible to be.

Centro Storico

B Caravaggio, piazza Riario Sforza 157, **T** 081-2110066, **F** 081-4421578, www.caravaggiohotel.it *Map 2, A7, p249* This new hotel (opened in December 2001) is a nice mix of old and new. All the rooms have at least some remnants of the building's 17th-century origins, be it exposed beams or parts of ancient arches, though the overall refurbishment is essentially modern. Rooms have all the facilities you'd expect from a four-star hotel though the bathrooms are rather small and have showers rather than baths. With just 11 rooms it's cosy feel and staff are amiable.

B **Neapolis**, via Francesco del Guidice 13, **T** 081-4420815, **F** 081-4420819 www.hotelneapolis.com *Just off piazza Pietra-Santa. Map 2, C4, p248* All rooms in this smart terracotta-tiled hotel have computers and some have balconies with views up to the Certosa di San Martino. Rooms are spacious and staff are very willing to help. The breakfast room is rather dark.

C **Europeo**, via Mezzocannone 109/c, **T/F** 081-5517254. *Not far from corso Umberto I and opposite the University. Map 2, G5, p248* This friendly little hotel has a distinct college feel to it. It's right in the liveliest part of the Centro Storico and though some rooms are on the small side all are well-kept and have en-suite bathrooms.

C **Sansevero**, Albergo Sansevero, via Santa Maria di Constantinopoli 101, **T** 081-210907, **F** 081-211698, www.albergosansevero.it *Just north of piazza Bellini. As all are in antique palazzi, this hotel (and Sansevero Degas and Soggiorno Sansevero, see below) are not allowed signs outside, so you'll need to find their bells beside the doors. Map 2, C2, p248* This is one of a group of three hotels all in fairly close proximity in the heart of the Centro Storico. All offer nicely furnished, large rooms in handsome old palazzi at a very good price. All are on, or just off, Naples' most pleasant piazzas. Many rooms have balconies with attractive views, and most have en-suite bathrooms. Well-placed for transport links. In the Albergo Sansevero breakfast is served in the bar downstairs.

C Sansevero Degas, Albergo Sansevero Degas, calata Trinità Maggiore 53 (piazza del Gesù), **T** 081-5511276. *Map 2, F1, p248* This is the second of a group of three hotels (see Albergo Sansevero above). Albergo Sansevero Degas is on piazza del Gesù, which can get quite noisy in the evenings, especially at weekends.

C Soggiorno Sansevero, Soggiorno Sansevero, piazza San Domenico Maggiore 9 (Palazzo Sansevero), **T** 081-5515742. *On the eastern side of the piazza. Map 2, D4, p248* The last of a group of three hotels (see Albergo Sansevero), in an attractive old building.

D Albergo Bellini, via San Paolo 44, **T** 081-456996, **F** 081-292256, www.export.it/hotelbellini *In a quiet side street north off via dei Tribunali. Map 2, B4, p248* This small, friendly, good-value hotel has a 1960s feel and is popular with travellers. Rooms are a reasonable size, beds are big andhave good bathrooms. The hotel is very conveniently near the centre of the Centro Storico.

D Hotel Duomo, via Duomo 228, **T** 081-265988. *Just north of San Gregorio Maggiore. Map 2, B/C4, p248* This welcoming little place is a bit dingy at present, though the owners have great plans to improve it. All rooms face the inner courtyard and so are quiet, despite being on via Duomo. It's well-placed and cheap.

E Imperia, piazza Luigi Miraglia 386, **T/F** 081-459347. *Just west of piazza Bellini. Map 2, C3, p248* Basic but very conveniently located, the fourth-floor Imperia has a kitchen for communal use and an amiable hostel atmosphere. One room has en-suite bathroom.

Via Toledo and the Quartieri Spagnoli

A Hotel Convento, via Speranzella 137/A, **T** 081-403977, **F** 081-400332, www.hotelilconvento.com *From via Toledo take via Tre Re a Toledo. Map 3, B/C3, p250* A well-restored 16th-century building. Very welcoming and fitted out with old, dark furniture, the place has a homely feel, though if you're unlucky you may get a cupid reproduction above your bed. All rooms have a/c and en-suite bathrooms. Some have baths and two rooms are specially designed for disabled users. The two suites at the top each have their own private roof garden and there is a family room with a mezzanine kids' floor.

B Hotel Toledo, via Montecalvario, 15, **T** 081-406800, **F** 081-406871. *Directly off via Toledo. Map 3, A4, p250* Pleasantly renovated (though the pictures in some rooms may not be to every-one's taste) this hotel is set far enough back from via Toledo to be reasonably quiet and still very central. Mod cons include satellite TV, radio, safes, a/c, en-suite bathrooms, free internet use and mini-bars. There is also a roof terrace with views over the Quartieri Spagnoli.

C Napolit'amo, via Toledo 148, **T/F** 081-5523626, www.napolitamo.it *Right on via Toledo itself, just north of the Municipio. The hotel is not signposted from outside the palazzo and the name on the bell (to the right of the door) is 'Centro Turistisco'. Map 3, A/B4, p250* In the handsome Palazzo Tocco di Montemiletto (once home to the prince of the same name) this is an excellent, family-run option. The large sunny rooms have high ceilings and many have balconies over the pedestrianized shopping street below. If you're lucky enough to get the room on the corner, it has two sets of large windows. Staff are friendly and helpful. Breakfast is at the bar down-stairs. There is free internet access and a garage.

E Albergo Spezia, 2 entrances, via Montecalvario, 41, and vico Santa Maria delle Grazie a Toledo, 2, **T** 081-407767. *Map 3, A3, p250* This conveniently situated but rather run-down hotel, just back from via Toledo (and hence potentially a little noisy), has good old rooms, some of them quite big. Though rooms have basins, none has a bathroom and some of communal bathrooms are poky.

G Messina, vico Luperano 7, **T** 081-5499958. *Just north of piazza Dante, off via E Pessina to the left.* Map 2, B1, p248 You would have to be very unfussy to want to stay here. It's not very friendly and has a minimum of facilities. Having said that, it is about the cheapest place in town, cheaper even than the youth hostel, and all rooms have basins and big beds. It's not badly placed either, near the Museo and piazza Dante, though in rather a dark street.

Corso Umberto I and around

B Hotel Suite Esedra, via Cantani 12, **T/F** 081-5537087. *Just off Corso Umberto I, directly south of the Ospedale Ascalesi.* Map 2, D9, p249 A tall, thin hotel, very convenient for the Centro Storico, as well as the central station. Though the surrounding area lacks the feel of the centre itself, inside a warm and more than averagely sophisticated atmosphere pervades the place. Small but well-equipped rooms, almost all with balconies, are decorated with frescoes (modern copies of old paintings), and a suite on the top floor has a roof terrace and pool. All rooms have a/c, bathrooms and TV.

B Nuovo Rebecchino, corso Garibaldi 356, **T** 081-35327, **F** 081-268026, www.napleshotels.it/nuovorebecchino *Just south of piazza Principe Umberto.* Map 2, A12, p249 Smart and efficient, the Nuovo Rebecchino claims about two-thirds of its clientele are tourists though it feels a bit like a conference hotel. Nevertheless, rooms are large, well-equipped and quiet if not especially cosy.

B Prati, via Cesare Rosarollo 4, **T** 081-268898, **F** 081-5541802. *On road leading northwest off piazza Principe Umberto.* Map 2, A12, p249 Far enough from piazza Garibaldi to feel civilized and decidedly less run-down, near enough to be convenient for transport links, the Prati has a disorganized and worn around the edges air but this is more than made up for by the eager and friendly service. Rooms are plain but there is a small roof terrace with views of sorts (between buildings) of Vesuvius, the sea and San Martino. Some rooms have terraces, others have balconies facing the street.

C Gallo, via S Spaventa 11, **T** 081-200512, **F** 081-201849. *On a street just off the southern side of piazza Garibaldi. Map 2, B12, p249* Clean and reasonably good value, this hotel has a slightly dated and uninspiring décor, rather reminiscent of Fawlty Towers. Rooms at least have bathrooms, TV and telephone.

C Ideal, piazza Garibaldi 99, **T** 081-269237, **F** 081-285942, www.albergoideal.it *On the southern side of the piazza. Map 2, B12, p249* One of the best options on the piazza, Hotel Ideal is welcoming, clean and simple without being too plain. All rooms have bathrooms with baths. Most also have balconies, though the views are hardly picturesque. Staff speak unusually good English.

C Tirreno, via G Pica, 20/22, **T** 081-5539277, **F** 081-5548752, www.hoteltirreno.com *South of piazza Garibaldi and east of via Garibaldi. Map 2, B12, p249* This hotel has friendly and professional staff and large, pleasant rooms with enormous beds. It's a block back from the piazza, which makes it quieter, though unfortunately no more salubrious. Rooms have a/c, bathrooms and TV.

D Nettuno, via Sedile di Porto 9, **T** 081-5510193. *Northwest of piazza G Bovio. Map 2, H3, p248* Basic but clean, the *Nettuno* has big beds and a bar in progress at the time of writing. Décor is fairly nastily modern, however, and though the position is good for sights the immediate area is less than exciting.

D Odeon, via S Spaventa 29, **T** 081-285656. *On a street just off the southern side of piazza Garibaldi. Map 2, C12, p249* All rooms here have bathrooms and TV and it's set far enough back from the piazza to be comparatively quiet. It has a rather hectic feel though, and there are other better budget options nearby.

E Eden, corso Novara 9, **T** 081-285344. *On the road off the north-east corner of piazza Garibaldi.* *Map 2, A12, p249* You get a warm welcome at this traveller-friendly hotel. The 45 rooms are basic but all have bathrooms. External rooms have limited views, internal ones are quieter. Many are generously large.

F Aurora, piazza Garibaldi 60, **T/F** 081-201920. *Between via Torino and via Milano on the north side of piazza Garibaldi.* *Map 2, A12, p249* Unhelpful but very cheap, this small hotel offers little in the way of facilities or service. Some rooms are en-suite and have views over the building site that is currently piazza Garibaldi.

F Clara, via San Biagio ai Taffettanari 7, **T** 081-5540104. *On a reasonably quiet street one back from corso Umberto I, just west of piazza N Amore.* *Map 2, E7, p249* This plain and simple pensione is nothing exceptional but is clean and very good value for money. Three of the 11 rooms are en-suite.

La Sanità and Capodimonte

A Villa Capodimonte, via Moiariello 66, **T** 081-459000, **F** 081-299344, villacap@tin.it *Up on the hill near Capodimonte itself, southeast of the Palazzo Reale.* This modern hotel (built in 1995) has a refined air which sets it apart from much of the competition down below in the city. Excellent views and gardens just about make up for its distance from the centre.

B Real Orto Botanico, via Foria 192, **T** 081-4421528, **F** 081-4421346, www.hotelcavournapoli.it *South of botanical gardens.* This new hotel (it opened in 2001) has views of the botanical gardens from its own roof garden. Tastefully decorated in beige and pale olive green, what it lacks in antique character it makes up for in immaculate cleanliness and efficiency. The double glazing does a good job of keeping out the noise of via Foria and most rooms have sofas and desks as well as heating and a/c. Breakfast is a generous buffet affair, and overall it's good value.

Chiaia, Mergellina and Posillipo

A Majestic, largo Vast a Chiaia 68, **T** 081-416500, F 081-410145, www.majestic.it *Just east of via G Carducci and north of piazza G Amendola.* Map 4, I6, p253 This large hotel is slightly orientated towards a business clientele, but is still a good place to stay. Well-located, it has very efficient and friendly service. Rooms on the top floors have good views over the rooftops of Chiaia to the Bay. It has all the facilities you would expect of a four-star hotel, from baby-sitting and a/c to internet provision.

B Ausonia, via Caracciolo 11, **T/F** 081-682278. *Right opposite the Mergellina hydrofoil port, and south of piazza J Sannazzaro.* Map 5, L4, p255 Handy for access to the islands, each room is accordingly given a nautical theme, complete with portholes and ship's tiller headboards, which may or may not appeal. Rooms all have bath-rooms, heating, a/c and TV. The hotel faces the inner courtyard of a palazzo, meaning the rooms are quiet but don't have great views.

B Canada, via Mergellina 43, **T** 081-680952, **F** 081-5785417. *Just south of piazzetta Leone a Mergellina.* Map 5, L4, p255 A fair way from the centre, but near bus, tram and funicular routes, some of the rooms here have excellent views over the marina of Mergellina and the bay beyond. The area has a good supply of bars, restaurants and gelaterie and it's also a convenient location for catching hydrofoils to the islands. Service can be unfriendly.

B Pinto Storey, via G Martucci 72, **T** 081-681260, **F** 081-667536. *North of Villa Pignatelli, south of piazza Amadeo.* Map 4, H3, p253 In the same building as the *Pensione Ruggiero*, and therefore very convenient, this pleasantly decorated hotel has a worn old-fashioned feel. Its staff can be decidedly unhelpful, however. All rooms have fans and some have a/c. All have TVs and safes. Bus and train tickets are available from reception.

C Pensione Ruggiero, via G Martucci 72, **T** 081-7612460, **F** 081-663536, hotelrug@libero.it *North of Villa Pignatelli, south of piazza Amadeo. Map 4, H3, p253* This welcoming hotel, spread over two floors (reception is upstairs), is excellently positioned in an attractive building in the middle of Chiaia. Rooms are simple but clean, and all but one have bathrooms. Some have views of the piazza. There is an enormous TV in the lounge area.

C Crispi, via F Crispi 104, **T/F** 081-668048. *Map 5, F8, p254* This no-frills hotel is not in a bad position and is clean and relatively cheap. Don't expect any smiles though. Most 'double beds' are in fact two singles pushed together. All rooms have bathrooms.

D Le Fontane al Mare, via N Tommaseo 14, **T** 081-7643470. *On the seafront between Castel dell'Ovo and the Villa Comunale. Map 3, J1, p251* This fourth-floor hotel has a creaky and slightly decrepit kind of charm. Small balconies and a breakfast room have views over the seafront and left to the castle. Some rooms are en-suite. The advertised 'Distinguished hospitality' may be a letdown, however.

F Ostello Mergellina, salita della Grotta a Piedigrotta 23, **T** 081-7612346, **F** 081-7612391. *Come out of Mergellina Metro station, turn right, right again under the railway bridge, and right again up a switchback road. Map 5, J2/3, p255* Naples' youth hostel is hardly in the best area of town, but it's relatively safe, and it's not far from the buzzing marina area of Mergellina. It's also right behind the mainline Mergellina train station (also a metro station) and so not at all badly connected. The hostel is clean and friendly and has double rooms as well as family rooms and dormitories, almost all with bathrooms. It's closed between 0030 and 0630.

Vomero

L Grand Hotel Parker's, corso V Emanuele 135, **T** 081-7612474,
F 081-663527, www.grandhotelparkers.it *Map 4, H1, p253* One of
Naples' oldest hotels, Parker's is a grand five-star hotel overlooking
Chiaia and the Bay. That is unless you get a room facing the sheer
rock face behind the hotel. Some of the luxuriousness has worn a little thin in places but the piano bar and roof terrace are a spectacular
place to have breakfast, dinner or just a drink.

A Britannique, corso V Emanuele 133, **T** 081-7614145,
F 081-660457. *Map 4, H1, p253* The *Britannique* has many fans,
and past visitors include Ibsen, Harold Macmillan and George Ber-
nard Shaw. There's a garden with palm trees, excellent views and
Empire-style furniture. The 'unaltered beauty of times past' the
hotel purports to embody, however, seems a little less charming
than it should, perhaps because of the conference facilities, or perhaps because it's all just a bit too British.

C Belvedere, via T Angelini 51/55, **T** 081-5788169,
F 081-5785417. *On a street leading northwest from Museo Certosa di
San Martino and opposite Castel Sant'Elmo. Map 4, B7, p252* High
above the city, just across the road from the Castel Sant'Elmo the
chief selling point of this hotel is, unsurprisingly, its views. Rooms
are modern and fairly characterless and bathrooms are pokey but
there's a garden with lemon trees and balconies that look
spectacularly across the rooftops of the city to Vesuvius.

Pozzuoli

G Campeggio Internazionale Vulcano Solfatara, via
Solfatara 161, Pozzuoli, **T** 081-5267413, F 081-5263482,
www.solfatara.it *The nearest campsite to Naples' city centre, the 152
bus passes by just outside the gates.* Right inside an ex-volcanic

crater, which still bubbles and hisses away through the trees (see p91 for more details). Apart from the possibility of the occasional whiff of sulphur drifting over, you wouldn't really know, however, and this is a very green and pleasant place to stay. There is a swimming pool and restaurant and it's also possible to rent bungalows with two, three or four beds.

Sorrento

STS Travel (piazza Tasso 3, **T** 081-8072433, **F** 081-8771755, www.syrene.it/scenictravel) has an enormous selection of brochures and can make bookings for Sorrento's myriad hotels.

L Excelsior Vittoria, piazza Tasso 34, **T** 081-8071044, **F** 081-8771206, www.excelsiorvittoria.com *Right in the heart of town: you can walk from piazza Tasso through the hotel's orange-tree filled park, past the outdoor swimming pool to reach it.* Almost all the rooms of Sorrento's five-star hotel have balconies, and most of them overlook the sea. The hotel is extremely elegantly furnished, there is a grand dining room with a frescoed ceiling and a large terrace with great views across the bay to Vesuvius. There's a 10-15% discount for low season.

B Villa di Sorrento, piazza Tasso/viale Caruso, **T** 081-8781068, **F** 081-8072679, info@belmaretravel.com *Just to the south of Sorrento's main square.* This amicable hotel is excellently placed. All rooms have a/c and terraces or balconies, though views are not spectacular. All have good bathrooms though some are small.

D Astoria, via Santa Maria delle Grazie 24, **T** 081-8074030, **F** 081-8071208. *In a quiet street in the old part of town.* An ideally placed and good-value, though slightly characterless, hotel. All rooms have bathrooms though they are rather pokey. There is a garden, which some rooms overlook.

Capri

LL Capri Palace, via Capodimonte 2b, Anacapri, **T** 081-978011, www.capri-palace.com The *Capri Palace* benefits from its slightly detached position on Anacapri. Less ostentatious and brash than competitors despite its situation on the site of one of Emperor Augustus's palaces, it is elegantly bedecked in whites, golds and international celebrities. Some suites have private hanging gardens and pools. Transfers or excursions by helicopter available on request.

LL Capri, via Roma 71, Capri Town, **T** 081-8370003, **F** 081-8378913, www.htlcapri.it The *Capri* has a slightly self-conscious air of faded grandeur to match its faded pink façade. Service is relaxed and all but four rooms have a sea view. The large restaurant downstairs is suitably grand.

A Belsito, via Matermania 9/11, **T** 081-8378750, **F** 081-8376622, www.hotelbelsito.com In an attractive wine and white painted 18th-century building just outside CapriTown with a great view, the friendly Belsito has bright rooms with balconies, a tree-shaded terrace and a decent restaurant with pizzas from a wood-fired oven and homemade pasta. Prices drop considerably out of season.

B La Prora, via Castello 6, **T/F** 081-8370281. *On an attractive and quiet road, halfway between the piazzetta and the Belvedere Cannone.* 'La Prora' means the bow of a ship, and the hotel does indeed stick out bow-like towards the sea. Though single rooms are cramped, on the whole this small, newly redecorated hotel is a joy to be in, and exceptionally friendly. From some balconies you can, on a clear day, see everything from Ischia to Vesuvius.

A Gatto Blanco, via V Emanuele 36/60, **T** 081-8370203, **F** 081-8378060. A good, gay-friendly option: a small hotel in a quiet area but with decent views.

C Villa Eva, via La Fabbrica 8, **T/F** 081-8372040, www.caprionline.com/villaeva *Between Anacapri and the Grotta Azzurra.* This good-value and easy going establishment has a swimming pool and is surrounded by greenery.

D La Reginella, via Matermania 36, **T/F** 081-8370500, lreginella@libero.it *In the hills and terraces above Capri Town.* This hotel has a great breakfast terrace with excellent views down the coast towards Marina Piccola. Views from the rooms are generally less spectacular. All rooms have bathrooms and some have baths.

Ischia

A Park Hotel Miramare, Giardini Termali Aphrodite Apollon, Sant'Angelo d'Ischia, **T** 081-999219, www.hotelmiramare.it The main attraction of this four star hotel are its thermal baths (see p106) to which guests have free access. Rooms also have good sea views, breakfast is on an attractive terrace and service is professional.

C Il Monastero, Castello Aragonese 3, Ischia Ponte, **T** 081-992435. The location of this small hotel, right inside the Aragonese castle, is hard to beat and the views are exceptional. The simple white and blue rooms, where monks once slept, are mostly en-suite. Half-board is obligatory and mealtimes inflexible.

D Casa Garibaldi, Madonnella, Sant'Angelo d'Ischia, **T** 081-999420. Beautifully situated among gardens high above the sea, with panoramic views east over the beaches of Maronti, this homely place is exceptionally well-equipped for the price, with pool, sauna, hydro-massage and a large communal kitchen. All rooms have bathrooms and some are apartments with kitchens.

E Locanda sul Mare, via Lasolino 90, Ischia Porte, **T/F** 081-981470, www.locandasulmare.it Open all year, this is a clean and light hotel, smarter on the inside than you might imagine from without, despite a slightly strange collection of modern art which decorates the corridor walls. All rooms are en-suite, and some have good views over the harbour.

Procida

A La Casa Sul Mare, via Salita Castello 13, **T/F** 081-8968799, www.lacasasulmare.it *Up the hill from the harbour in Coricella.* A more attractive or better value-for-money hotel than this is hard to imagine (prices drop sharply out of season). Small enough to be friendly and homely, but elegant and well-equipped enough to be worthy of its four stars. All the rooms in this exceptional hotel have a terracotta-tiled terrace looking out over the beautiful harbour of Corricella. The interior is coolly decorated with white tiles, the furniture is simple but classy. Breakfast is served in a small garden.

C Albergo del Faro, via Faro 40, **T** 081-8969306/8969497, **F** 081-8101791, www.procida.net/villadelfaro *Hidden away among lemon groves near the end of a road in the northeast of the island.* Albergo del Faro is certainly quiet and is perfectly pleasant but might be too far away from the rest of civilization, though it does have its own restaurant.

D Hotel Celeste, via Rivoli 6, **T** 081-8967488, **F** 081-8967670, www.campnet.it/celeste *Near the southern end of the island, set back from the marina of Chiaiolella.* This friendly, sprawling open-plan place has a variety of rooms, the best of which have excellent sea views and pleasant terraces, the worst of which are windowless and pokey. There's a young, bubbly atmosphere to the place and a decent restaurant with a proper woodfired pizza oven.

G Camping There are a number of campsites, mostly around the centre of the island. *Camping Vivara*, via IV Novembre, just off via

Vittorio Emanuele, near the junction with via Lavadera, **T** 081-8969242 (**T** 081-5560529 if campsite is closed), is well-placed for the beach and excellent beach restaurant at Chiaia. There is a bar on-site, 30 camping places and two bungalows.

Positano

L Palazzo Murat, via dei Mulini 23, **T** 089-875177, F 089-811419, www.starnet.it/murat/welcome.html   The Murat has two wings, one antique, and one 'new', though even the new part is not so new, and is certainly not modern in style, though it has been recently renovated. The antique part of the hotel is exceedingly classy: rooms are enormous with antique furniture and flowery balconies looking out over the orange-tree-filled courtyard below and Positano beyond. The restaurant downstairs, and in the courtyard, offers such delicacies as guinea fowl with lemon-flavoured honey. Classical concerts are also held in the courtyard.

B Pupetto, via Fornillo 37, **T** 089-875087, **F** 089-811517, www.hotelpupetto.it   This excellently situated hotel, at the back of Fornillo beach, also has a good restaurant. All rooms are en-suite and all have balconies with sea views "where to spend unforgettable moments". The style is a little too modern to be as romantic as it would like to be, but when you can practically roll out of bed onto the beach in the morning this may not be such a problem.

B Albergo Santa Caterina, via Pasitea 113, **T/F** 089-875019. Slightly ragged around the edges, but very affable, the Santa Caterina is high above the beach and has rooms with good views. It's worth trying to barter on room rates, especially out of season.

C La Bouganville, via C Colombo 25, **T** 089-875047, **F** 089-811150, www.bouganville.it   Though far from being Positano's worst hotel, La Bouganville is one of its cheapest. All rooms are en-suite and rooms with sea views (for which you pay approximately €15 extra) have terraces. It's also near the beach.

Amalfi

AL Luna Convento, via Pantaleone Comite 33, **T** 089-871002, F 089-871333, www.amalficoast.it/hotel/luna *Perched on the cliff at the eastern end of Amalfi* . The setting for this hotel is stunning: an ex-convent set around a cloister founded by St Francis in 1222 in which you can opulently laze the day away. There is a pool half-way down the cliffs, a splendid dining room, another restaurant in the Saracen Tower on the other side of the road, and the whole place feels very relaxed in its tiled and whitewashed luxuriousness.

A Antica Repubblica Amalfi, vico dei Pastai 2, **T** 089-8736310, **F** 089-871926, www.starnet.it/anticarepubblica *Just north of piazza del Duomo*. With a large terrace and flowery balconies, the restored hotel serves a good buffet breakfast and has tastefully furnished rooms overlooking the main street.

B Sole, largo della Zecca 2, **T** 089-871147, www.starnet.it/hsole *Set in a quiet courtyard from where a covered passageway takes you to the piazza del Duomo*. The *Hotel Sole* is friendly, has light rooms and is reasonably modern in style. All rooms have bathrooms. A good-value option, especially out of season.

C Lidomare, largo Duchi Piccolomini 9, **T** 089-871332, **F** 089-871394, www.lidomare.it *On the quiet piazza dei Dogi to the west of piazza Duomo*. The *Lidomare*'s exceptionally welcoming owners are obviously proud of their hotel and rightly so. The hotel has character: half the rooms overlook the sea and have small terraces adorned with geraniums. Safes, a/c and fridges are all standard and there are even jacuzzis in some rooms. Probably the best value for money anywhere on the Amalfi Coast.

G Scalinatella, piazza Umberto I 5/6, **T/F** 089-871492, www.amalficoast.it/hotel/scalinatella *The Scalinatella is actually in neighbouring Atrani, just off the piazza.* As near as Amalfi gets to a hostel, the place is basic but cheap and has washing machines and a midnight curfew. They also organize more expensive private rooms and apartments around Atrani.

Ravello

L Villa Cimbrone, via Santa Chiara 26, **T** 089-857459/ 089-858072, **F** 089-857777, villacimbrone@amalfinet.it *Open mid-Mar-end Nov.* This exceedingly smart hotel offers the opportunity to follow in the footsteps of famous guests from times past such as Keynes, Churchill, Forster and Greta Garbo (who eloped here) by staying in the Villa Cimbrone itself. A stay here also allows a wander around the beautiful gardens after the coach parties have gone. The hotel itself is fitted out in immaculately luxurious style without ever being overly ornate: there are lots of tiles, antique furniture and tall windows which of course all have amazing views, either over the gardens or the sea. There's even a helipad for those who don't fancy taking the bus.

A Giordano, via Santa Chiara 2, **T** 089-857255/089-857170, **F** 089-857071. *Closed Jan-Mar but Villa Maria Ravello open all year round. Near centre of town.* This friendly and helpful place is complete with a swimming pool. It's slightly more modern than its sister hotel *Villa Maria Ravello* nearby (same contact details) but has a pleasant ambience, high ceilings, tiles and impressive potted ferns.

D Villa Amore, via dei Fusco 5, **T/F** 089-857135. *Near Villa Cimbrone, a 10 minute walk away from the centre.* This friendly, popular and cheap hotel has balconies opening onto a garden with great views, where you can have breakfast overlooking the sea far below. Rooms are basic but adequate and en-suite. Book ahead.

Eating and drinking

Eating is a big deal in Naples. Portions are copious, vegetables and fish are almost always fresh and local and though the cuisine tends to be steadfastly simple and traditional, it is an element of city life of which Neapolitans are very proud. Meals start late and keep going, though the three-hour lunches of old are becoming increasingly confined to Sundays. Many smaller trattorie and osterie specialize in excellent lunches, some not opening in the evenings at all, but its not at all unusual to leave a restaurant after midnight and still find people streaming in.

Naples' cuisine is excellent but best when its not complicated. Many of the city's bigger and smarter restaurants merely serve a blander version of what you find in the cheaper and more interesting trattorie, which are where the city's culinary heart lies. You can find good food all over the city, but the Centro Storico and the maze of the Quartieri Spagnoli hide the most gems. The same can be true in the surrounding areas where small places by the sea serve delicious and very fresh seafood.

The **pizza** (see also next page) is a Neapolitan symbol worshipped by the city's inhabitants, alongside San Gennaro and Maradona, and it's true that they are not made quite as well anywhere else. A genuine Neapolitan pizza has a chewy rather than a crunchy crust, and the thinner, Roman version is pretty much sacrilege here.

A pizza is often eaten as a whole meal on its own, whereas with other meals the norm is to have a first course (*primo*) often pasta or soup) followed by a main course (*secondo*), usually just a simple meat dish. You need to order your vegetables as a separate dish (*contorno*). The main course is often something you can construct yourself from a fairly wide choice of meats and vegetables. This may be on display, so you can go and point at what you want. Before any of this you can also have a starter (*antipasto*) and then at the end you can round it all off with a dessert (*dolce*).

Many places **around the bay** have decidedly limited eating options. In Baia you're probably best off grabbing a piece of pizza or two from *Pizza Village* opposite the station or taking a picnic. Cuma has no more than a small café. Pompeii and Ercolano both have some reasonable, if touristy, options outside the ruins but you may have problems if you want to go out and re-enter afterwards. In any case, both places make excellent picnic spots.

Cafés, and especially coffee, are another vital component of Neapolitan life. Most also serve alcohol, though locals come more for the coffee, and the pastries.

Eating and drinking

Pizzas

To be honest it's hard to find a really bad pizza in Naples. The city that invented the things is proud of its culinary heritage, and guards its traditions almost obsessively. Even fast food pizza-by-the-slice joints do what would, anywhere else in the world, be considered a very high-class pizza.

There is even an association, *Associazione Vera Pizza Napoletana* (Neapolitan True Pizza Association), which protects the ideals of a good pizza. These include: dough made only of flour, water, yeast and salt, which must be left to rise for at least six hours; a hot wood-burning oven; and raw, simple, high-quality ingredients. At its most puritanical (see *Da Michele* p154) this means having only two types of pizza on the menu: Margherita and Marinara.

Whereas around the world a **Marinara** may often have seafood on, the true Neapolitan Marinara (so-called because it was the meal fishermen would take out with them for the day

on their boats) is about as plain as they get, with a topping of only tomato, oregano, garlic and oil. A **Margherita**, on the other hand, as invented (so they claim) by *Pizzeria Brandi* (p147) for Queen Margherita of Italy, has the national colours of red (tomato), green (basil) and white (mozzarella). In many places you will find that there are subtle variations on this classic: a speciality of *Trianon*, for example, is the **pizza DOC** (Denominazione di Origine Controllata), with mini mozzarella di bufala (the 'proper' mozzarella, made from buffalo milk) and cherry tomatoes. Similar is the **Filetto**, with sliced fresh tomatoes. Other toppings which are tolerated are olives, anchovies, ricotta, sausage, *friarielli* (similar to broccoli), *rucola* (rocket, also called rughetta) and *prosciutto crudo* (Parma ham). Seafood combined with cheese, on the other hand, is almost as much of a *faux pas* as pineapple.

Santa Lucia

Restaurants

€€€ **Amici Miei**, via Monte di Dio 78, **T** 081-7646063. *Tue-Sat 1230-1530, 1930-0000, Sun 1230-1530, closed Mon. Map 3, G2, p251* In this yellow-walled and wooden-beamed restaurant, often full of smart families, the emphasis is on meat rather than fish. Some very good homemade pastas include a dish with provola (a kind of smoked mozzarella), sweet chillies and cherry tomatoes.

€€€ **Bersagliera**, borgo Marinari 10, **T** 081-7646016. *1200-1530, 1930-2330, closed Tue and Jan. Map 3, K5, p251* Possibly the best of borgo Marinari's smart restaurants, Salvador Dali and Sophia Loren have both eaten here by the waterside. La Bersagliera concentrates on seafood and doesn't do anything too adventurous.

€€€ **Brandi**, salita Sant'Anna di Palazzo 1/2, **T** 081-416928, www.brandi.it *1230-1500, 1930-0100. Map 3, F3, p250* Pizzeria Brandi, just off via Chiaia, is especially proud of its long history (it was founded in 1780) and, above all, its invention of the now ubiquitous pizza Margherita. The first such pizza was made for Queen Margherita on a visit to Naples in 1889. On subsequent visits she would apparently call for the pizza-makers of Brandi who would arrive at the gates of the Palace of Capodimonte with ingredients loaded onto a donkey and cart. Luckily, however, the restaurant does not put all its energy into resting on its laurels, and its pizzas continue to be excellent. It also does a good selection of other traditional Neapolitan food, and the *fritto misto* is particularly good.

€€€ **Cantinella**, via Cuma 42, **T** 081-7648684. *Mon-Sat 1230-1500, 1930-0100. Map 3, I5, p251* Considered by some to be Naples' best restaurant, the elegant *La Cantinella* tries to do something a

★ **Five of the best local wines**

Best

1 **Falangina** A very drinkable white, probably Campania's most popular wine.

2 **Biancolella** From Ischia, a dry white recommended as an accompaniment to *mozzarella di bufalo*.

3 **Greco di Tufo** Another good dry white, best drunk young.

4 **Aglianico del Taburno** One of the best reds from one of Campania's most established grapes. The *Aglianico* grape is also used to make the decent Taurasi.

5 **Lacrima Cristi del Vesuvio** Made from grapes grown on the fertile slopes of Vesuvius, this red is dark and rich.

little different to traditional Neapolitan cooking and usually pulls it off. The seafood is undoubtedly the highlight.

€€ **Marino**, via Santa Lucia 118/120, **T** 081-7640280, www.napoli.com/marino *Tue-Sun 1230-1530, 1930-0100. Halfway between piazza del Plebiscito and Marina Marinari. Map 3, J4, p251* This unassuming-looking place is a safe bet and popular with locals. The menu is too comprehensive for anything to be considered a real speciality, athough the seafood fritture are especially good.

€€ **Uva Nera**, via Gennaro Serra 29, **T** 081-7645485. *Tue-Sun 1230-1530, 2000-0000. Up the hill behind piazza del Plebiscito. Map 3, G3, p251* This friendly little restaurant specializes in rice and its risottos are excellent. Some of its fish dishes are a little bland, however. There is a good, fixed-price lunch (€9). Some of the effect of the attractive interior wears off when you realize that many of the tiles around the walls aren't real!

€ **Osteria della Mattonella**, via G Nicotera 13, **T** 081-416541. *Mon-Sat 1300-1500, 1930-2330. Tucked away up the hill from the* *piazza del Plebiscito. You may need to knock on the door and wait to be let in.* Map 3, F2, p250 This small traditional osteria is a gem, and popular with locals. The upstairs is beautifully decorated with antique tiles (*mattonella* means tile). The larger space downstairs is less atmospheric but there are plans to tile parts of this too. Fast, friendly and informal service is combined with fairly basic but delicious Neapolitan fare. An antipasto of fried mozzarella and aubergine with bacon, followed by spaghetti and washed down with a large beer will set you back about €10.

€ **Da Ettore**, via Santa Lucia 56, **T** 081-7640498. *1300-1530, 1930-0000. Between piazza del Plebiscito and borgo Marinari.* Map 3, I4, p251 Despite the Lowenbrau-branded chairs, the peach tablecloths and the slightly brusque service this is an excellent restaurant with a bubbling atmosphere and delicious food. The feel and the prices are more like those you'd expect to find well-hidden up a dark Neapolitan backstreet rather than on this main road. Both pizza and pasta are good, as are the *fritture*. The *parmigiana di melanzane* (layered and baked aubergine, mozzarella and tomato) is excellent.

€ **Da Peppino**, 18 via Solitaria, **T** 081-7644449. *Mon-Sat 0930-1630, 1930-0100. Tucked up a narrow washing-bedecked street behind piazza del Plebiscito.* Map 3, H3, p251 A plain local restaurant serving excellent local food. Conversation is standardly loud Neapolitan and even if you speak Italian you may feel like an outsider.

€ **Da Pietro**, via Luculliana 27, borgo Marinari, **T** 081-8071082. *Tue-Sun 1200-1500, 1900-2330.* Map 3, L4, p251 This wonderful little place in Borgo Marinari facing the water and Naples' poshest hotels feels slightly like an impostor. The menu is steadfastly limited, and you will probably be served by a man in a cloth cap while all around you in the neighbouring restaurants bow-ties and waistcoats are the order of the day. The seafood (there's often little else) is excellent and the house wine isn't at all bad either.

Cafés and pasticcerie

Bar Gambrinus, via Chiaia 1 (piazza Trieste e Trento), **T** 081-417582. *0800-0130. Map 3, F4, p250* The €0.80 it will cost you to enjoy a coffee at this most refined of Naples' bars is worth it just for the luscious interior and the photo opportunity. They also sell exceedingly good cakes and pastries, and not bad ice-creams either.

Bar Rosati, piazza Trieste e Trento 47, **T** 081-421660. *0730-0100. Not far from Bar Gambrinus on piazza Trieste e Trento. Map 3, E4, p250* Much less ostentatious than its near neighbour, this café does equally good coffees and arguably better sfogliatelle. They also specialize in Caffè Rocher (see box opposite).

La Sfogliatella Mary, Galleria Umberto I 66, **T** 081-402218. *Mon 0800-1430, Tue-Sat 0800-2030. By the via Toledo exit from Galleria Umberto. Map 3, D4, p250* This little stand has a seemingly constant supply of fresh hot sfogliatelle coming out of its oven, and usually a queue waiting for them.

Gelaterie

Gelateria Scimmia, piazza Trieste e Trento 54, **T** 081-410322. *0730-0000, closed Wed Sep-Apr*; piazza Carità 4, **T** 081-5520272. *1000-0000, closed Wed Sep-Apr. Map 3, E4, p250* The marketing line for Gelateria Scimmia is, "The gelateria that's in the hearts of all Neapolitans." Its produce must be in quite a lot of their stomachs too, because it does indeed have a good reputation around these parts. The bigger branch on piazza Carità is particularly good. The other, on piazza Trieste e Trento, is also a café, and serves good cakes, though not always the biggest or most original choices of ice-cream.

► Caffè and pasticcerie

The best coffee places will give you a glass of water with your coffee, in order to help you clear your palate.

Coffee

espresso/'normale' strong espresso, even by Italian standards
macchiato espresso with a touch of milk (literally 'marked', or 'stained')
lungo slightly less strong espresso
lungo macchiato as above but again with a touch of milk
latte macchiato the reverse of a standard macchiato, mainly milk with a touch of coffee
caffè corretto espresso with a dash of alcohol, usually grappa.
cappuccino a frothy, milky coffee never drunk after midday, usually with cocoa sprinkled on top
caffè latte a milkier less frothy version of the cappuccino
caffè nocciola coffee with a thick creamy hazelnut concoction
espresso Braziliano frothy milky topping with cocoa. Occasionally with a dash of alcohol
caffè Rocher coffee with hazelnuts and chocolate
Mostly espressos come *amaro* (without sugar) though you will generally be expected to add some. Milkier coffees often come with sugar already added. Ask for them amaro to avoid this.

Pasticcerie

Naples' pastries are legendary, particularly *sfogliatelle*, a light pastry crust enclosing a creamy ricotta-based filling. It is said here that 'There are three good things about Naples: the sun, the sea and the sfogliatelle.' Another saying says, '*Il Caffè e il Baba sono una cosa seria*' (coffee and rum baba are serious things).
The ubiquitous fried savouries (fritture) are pretty good too, and equally filling.

Dolci

sfogliatelle riccia flaky pastry with heavy ricotta-based filling

sfogliatelle frolla as above but with shortcrust pastry

graffe like doughnuts but supposedly lighter. You may not be able to tell the difference

sciu profiteroles

babà rum baba, usually seriously sweet, and dripping with syrup. Not easy to eat on the move.

cornetto con crema like a sweet croissant filled with custard, these are particularly good with the morning's first coffee. Also available plain

torta caprese a heavy and rich hazelnut and chocolate cake

Gelato

Ice-cream in Naples is usually very good, with a wide range of choices. In Sorrento and on the Amalfi Coast it can be even better. *Produzione artigianale* means the ice-cream is homemade. *Produzione proprio* means the ice-cream is homemade on the premises. You will have a choice of *coppa* (cup) or *cono* (cone), both at various different sizes. Ask either by size (*grande, medio, piccolo*) or by price.

Flavours vary from one place to the next, but some of the most popular you're likely to find are:

nocciola hazelnut

limone lemon

cioccolato chocolate

stracciatella pieces of chocolate in vanilla

amareno cherry

frutti di bosco mixed 'forest' fruits

fragola strawberry

marrone chestnut

bacio chocolate and nut (from Italian sweet of the same name)

zuppa Inglese trifle

Centro Storico

Restaurants

€€€ **Ristorante e Pizzeria Bellini**, via Costantinapoli 79/80,
T 081-459774. *Mon-Sun 1200-0100. Map 2, C2, p248* A well-
established and popular restaurant which serves very good seafood,
as well as reasonable pizzas, although the service can be slow and
unfriendly. The ubiquitous *spaghetti alle vongole* is excellent here.

€€ **Anema e Cozze**, piazza del Gesù 26/27, **T** 081-5518427.
Mon-Sun 1200-0000. Map 2, F2, p248 This well-placed restaurant-
cum-café (on the edge of piazza del Gesù) does a surprisingly good
pizza, as well as a decent fixed-price menu, and is an excellent place
to while away a few hours in the sun watching the world go by,
though its clientele is more tourist-based than local.

€€ **un SorRiso Integrale**, vico San Pietro a Majella 6, (piazza
Bellini) **T** 081-455026. *Mon-Sat 1300-1500, from May-August also Sun.
Thu and Sat also 2030-0030 with live music. Set back from main piazza,
in a small courtyard off the southeast corner. Map 2, D2, p248* This
organic vegetarian restaurant specializing in "Mediterranean,
Oriental and Parthenopean" food is friendly, if self-consciously
alternative. A "Mixed Plate", a satisfying mixture of the four or five
dishes of the day, will fill you up for about €7. There are occasional
special evenings of ethnic music with food to match.

€ **La Cantina di Via Sapienza**, via Sapienza 40/41,
T 081-459078. *Mon-Sat 1200-1530. Map 2, B3, p248* This popular
lunch-only local restaurant may not look like much from outside, but
you descend down into a simple, but pleasingly decorated place,
with fresh flowers on the tables and great food on the plates. A
delicious bowl of *Penne Aum Aum*, with aubergine, tomato and

mozzarella, is only €2.90. A combination plate of *contorni misti* (you can specify whether you'd prefer fried, fresh or vegetarian etc) is similarly good value. If you get there much after 1300 you may have to wait for a table.

€ **L'Antica Spaghetteria**, via Paladino 7, **T** 339-7085522. *Mon-Sun 1200-1530, Fri and Sat also 1900-0100. Map 2, D5, p248* Service is very quick in this busy restaurant, which serves a much more varied menu than its name suggests. There is a decent *menu turistico*, and a good selection of traditional Neapolitan fare. The piped radio can make it a little hectic though.

€ **Antica Osteria Pisano**, piazzetta Crocelle ai Mannesi 1-4, **T** 081-5548325. *1200-1530, 1930-late, closed Sun. Just south of the Duomo. Map 2, C7, p249* This small osteria is more visitor-friendly than some. It has a menu for a start. The food is still very Neapolitan, however. Good gnocchi or pasta dishes are followed by an excellent selection of *secondi piatti* and mouth-watering homemade desserts.

€ **Campagnola**, via dei Tribunali 47, **T** 081-459034. *Mon-Sun 1200-1600. Map 2, C4/5, p248* This trattoria in the centre of the Centro Storico spurns almost all of the usual restaurant niceties: you may have to write your own tab from a chalked menu on the wall; antipasti and first courses may all come at the same time; and (horror of horrors) there are no serviettes. The food is excellent, however, if simple and the atmosphere is informal and fun.

€ **Da Michele**, via Sersale 1, **T** 081-5539204. *1000-0000, closed Sun. Map 2, C9, p249* The purists' pizzeria supreme, this place has no pretensions at all, as if to say: "Look, all our energies are channelled into making the most perfect pizza possible". The menu has only two choices: Margherita or Marinara, and service is lightning quick. Even so, you'll probably have to wait to get in, but it will be worth it. *Da Michele* has a ticket system for waiting.

€ **Di Matteo**, via dei Tribunali 94, **T** 081-455262. *Mon-Sat 1000-0000*. *Map 2, B6, p248* Probably Naples' most popular take-away, pizza-by-the-slice joint, you can also sit down here to savour excellent pizzas.

€ **Trianon**, via Colletta 46, **T** 081-5539426. *Mon-Sun 1100-1500, 1830-2300*. *Map 2, C9, p249* On several floors (you may have to fight your way up the stairs through the crowds), this slightly chaotic restaurant is worth the effort to get one of their pizzas, which come in three sizes. You come for the food not the service, though.

€ **Lombardi a Santa Chiara**, via Benedetto Croce 59, **T** 081-5520780. *Tue-Sun 1200-1600, 2000-0000*. *Map 2, E3, p248* Service can be excruciatingly slow and somewhat eccentric at this Neapolitan institution but the pizzas are excellent and just about worth waiting for.

€ **Pizzeria dell'Angelo**, piazzetta Nilo 16, **T** 081-5422001. *Mon-Sat 1200-1600, 1900-0000*. *Map 2, D4, p248* A popular meeting place, this buzzing restaurant has a slightly commercial air to it, but does unfailingly good pizzas. It also serves them by the slice from outside if you don't have the time to sit down.

€ **Pizzi Cotto**, via Mezzocannone 129, **T** 081-5516291. *Mon-Sun 1200-1600, 1900-2300*. *Map 2, E4, p248* This welcoming little place isn't one of Naples' better-known pizzerie but its *pummarò* (fresh tomatoes, rucola and mozzarella) is excellent, and you're likely to get a table without too much trouble. It also does good antipasti.

Cafés and pasticcerie

Letterario Intra Moenia, piazza Bellini 70, **T** 081-290720, www.intramoenia.it *Mon-Sun 1000-0200*. *Map 2, C2, p248* A Neapolitan institution, this literary café has a decent menu and a cultured atmosphere. The big salads are good, though not cheap, and there's an unusually large selection of teas, as well as cocktails. They publish and sell some good maps and guides, mainly of the surrounding Centro Storico, alongside interesting photography books and postcards. Exhibitions, literary meetings, concerts and poetry evenings happen here and there's also internet access.

Scaturchio, vico San Geronimo alle Monache 5, **T** 081-5519815. *Mon, Wed-Sun 0730-2030, closed Tue. Map 2, E4, p248* On the south side of piazza San Domenico Maggiore, but with tables in the piazza itself, this place is well-known for its particularly good sfogliatelle. The range of other cakes and pastries on show may tempt you to come back for something else later.

Via Toledo and the Quartieri Spagnoli

Restaurants

€€ **Dante e Beatrice**, piazza Dante 44/45, **T** 081-5499438. *Tue-Sun 1200-1500, 0730-2300. Map 2, D1, p248* The homemade *orecchiette* ('little ears' of pasta) are good, as is the bean soup. Generally, though, it's fairly standard Neapolitan fare. What makes this place worth a visit is its excellent position on the sparklingly new piazza Dante: the outside tables are a great place from which to watch the world go by.

€ **Trattoria Casillo Enzo**, vico Rosario a Portamedina 25, **T** 081-5522248. *Mon-Sat 1200-1700.* A gem of a restaurant so well-hidden that its name isn't on display, inside or out. In fact from the outside there's not even much evidence of the fact that it's a restaurant at all. It certainly doesn't have a menu, and the interior is far from elegant, though the range on offer is surprisingly large. Add to that the excellence and cheapness of the food and the hospitality and you're onto a winner. You can sit and watch the family cook in front of you and if there's something you want that they aren't offering, they'll probably do it for you specially.

€ **Trattoria Nennella**, vico Lungo Teatro Nuovo 103-105. *Mon-Fri 1200-1500. Map 3, A3, p250* This excellent little trattoria a couple of blocks back from via Toledo is nearly always full at lunchtimes, so either get here early or be prepared to wait for a table. It is traditional to get a generous helping of Neapolitan jokes with your meal.

€ **Trattoria e Pizzeria Fratelli Prigiobbo**, via Portacarrese 96. *Mon-Sat 1200-2300. Map 3, B3, p250* This is fast food Neapolitan style: the décor of this slightly cramped trattoria is pretty nasty, and you may not find it very relaxing. The food is superb, however. Pizzas, pasta dishes and fish are all equally delicious, and very cheap. It is usually busy at lunchtimes. €9.50 for pasta, fish and beer.

€ **Lo Spacco**, vico Corrieri 37, **T** 081-5510203. *1200-1500. In a small street off via Santa Brigida. Map 3, C4, p250* Here you can sit at tables outside and eat delicious pasta dishes starting from €2.10, or fish from €3.10. The atmosphere is very friendly and you may also be able to pick up a very cheap pair of designer shoes from a man selling them on the pavement opposite.

€ **7 Soldi**, vico Tre Re 6, **T** 081-418727. *Tue-Sun 1200-1600, 1900-0100. Map 3, C4, p250* Queues for take-away pizzas form inside this welcoming place but the range of pastas and seafood is just as good. The risotto is unusually tasty for southern Italy, though the chef may take it into his head to add unexpected delicacies if he feels like it.

€ **Port'Alba**, via Port'Alba 18, **T** 081-459713. *1200-1600, 1800-0100. Map 2, D1, p248* What may be the world's oldest pizzeria (several sources say so though the restaurant itself makes admirably little fuss about it) was founded in 1738 and is also a fine restaurant which does an unusually generous fish salad. And you can eat outside under the Port'Alba itself. The pizzas alone are good and cheap enough to explain its extraordinary longevity.

Cafés and pasticcerie

Caffè Mexico, piazza Dante 86, **T** 081-5499330. *Mon-Sat 0730-2030. Map 2, D1, p248* Despite the name, this is a very Neapolitan café, with a reputation for its coffee which is second to none. The secret, so they say, is in the fact that the beans are roasted on the premises. If you're convinced, you can also buy some beans to take home with you. There are a couple of other branches around town.

Pintauro, via Toledo 275, **T** 081-417339. *Mon-Sat 0900-2030. Map 3, D4, p250* This pasticceria on via Toledo does very good cakes and pastries – an ideal place for a break from the exertions of shopping.

Gelaterie

Fantasia Gelati, there are three branches of this reliably good gelateria: via Cilea 80, **T** 081-5607001; via Toledo 381, **T** 081-5511212 and piazza Vanvitelli 22, **T** 081-5788383. All *Mon-Sun 0700-0000.*

Chiaia, Mergellina and Posillipo

Restaurants

€€€ **Rosiello**, via Santo Strato 10, Posillipo, **T** 081-7691288. *1230-1600, 1900-0000, closed Wed. At the top of via Marechiaro. It's a fair trek from Mergellina, but a fairly easy bus ride (140 goes here from* *the centre)*. This classy and romantic restaurant has a lilac-covered terrace with a great view over terraces and villas to the sea. The antipasti are particularly recommended: *calamaretti* (little calamari) or octopus salad are both very good, as is the mozzarella, tomato and rocket salad. They also serve pizzas in the evening.

€€ **Da Pasqualino**, piazza Sannazzaro 77-79, Mergellina, **T** 081-681524. *Wed-Mon 1200-1600, 1900-0000, closed Tue. Map 5, L4, p255* The enormous popularity of this place becomes clear at weekends and on holidays, when the large seating area outside becomes jam-packed with Neapolitans, another horde circling around waiting for a table. Service can be painfully slow, especially at these times, but the pizzas and the atmosphere are hard to beat.

€€ **Donna Margherita**, vico II Alabardieri 4-6, Chiaia, **T** 081-400129. *Mon-Sun 1230-1500. Map 4, J8, p253* In a slightly more picturesque setting than most Neapolitan restaurants, complete with palm-fringed garden, Donna Margherita serves a good mix of pasta and fish dishes alongside decent pizzas. There is usually a choice of two set menus (two courses plus mineral water) for €6.20.

€€ **Umberto**, via Alabardieri 30/31, Chiaia, **T** 081-418555. *Tue-Sun 1230-1600, 1900-0100. Map 4, J8, p253* Excellent pizzas and a good range of antipasti (including seafood salad and a mixed plate of fried Neapolitan delicacies) are the highlights of this smart restaurant. Alongside all the Neapolitan favourites there is a good choice of more original pizza toppings, and if you make up another good one for them they may put it in their Proposta da Voi (proposed by you) section. There's even a pizza Gobaciov (sic) (with cream, salmon and provola), presumably a reference to his head…

€€ **La Cantina di Albi Cocca**, via Ascensione 6, Chiaia, **T** 081-411658. *Tue-Sat 1200-1500, 2015-0000, Sun 1200-1500.*

Map 4, J4, p253 Don't let the large bright yellow signs outside put you off. Inside is a charming restaurant with excellent food and good service. Better-known for its extensive wine and beer menu (it's worth coming for this alone), the food here is also delicious. A huge range of pastas (try the *orecchiette* with chillies, olives and cherry tomatoes) can be followed by a good choice of meat, fish and vegetables. And you'll probably get bruschetta to start with as a part of your cover charge. In the evenings it can fill up and it may be worth booking, but at lunchtime you can expect relative peace and quiet.

€€ **Vini e Cucina**, corso V Emanuele 762, **T** 081-660302. *Mon-Sun 1030-1530, 1900-2330.* Opposite Mergellina railway station, this is a good place for traditional Neapolitan food: the pasta is reasonable and the seafood is better. But save some room for the torta Caprese (dense chocolate and hazelnut cake) which is exquisite. The house white wine is best avoided.

€ **La Botte**, vico Satriano 8, Chiaia, **T** 081-7647337. *Mon-Sat 1330-1500, 2000-2300.* *Map 4, K7, p253* Half wine bar, half trattoria, this atmospheric little place does a good selection of food to go with your wine, from snacks to a full-blown meal.

€ **Trattoria da Antonio**, vico II Alabardieri 30, Chiaia, **T** 081-407147. *Mon-Sat 1200-1600, 1930-0100.* *Map 4, J8, p253* This small and simple friendly trattoria does a good range of traditional Neapolitan fare. A generous bowl of pasta and lentils with wine is only €5.

€ **Vinarium**, via Cappella Vecchia 7, Chiaia, **T** 081-7644114. *Mon-Fri 1030-1430, Mon-Sat 1900-0230.* *Map 4, K8, p253* A busy and informal atmosphere helps make this a very pleasant place to eat and drink. The food is simple rather than inspired though there are some decent salads and rice dishes. The range of wines is far from simple, however, and the opening hours are very sociable.

€ **Trattoria da Cicciotto**, Calata Ponticello a Marechiato, Posillipo, **T** 081-5751165. *Mon-Sun 1200-1600, 2000-0100.* Spilling onto the street right by the sea in Marechiaro, this is a popular and friendly spot a world away from the rigours of Naples. Traditional Neapolitan food with some excellent fish dishes.

€ **Matozzi**, via Filangieri 16, **T** 081-416378. *Mon-Sat 1300-1500, 2000-0000.* *Map 4, I8, p253* The antipasti here are nearly as generous as the pizza toppings, which are delicious if a little on the heavy side. If you're up to the challenge, try the excellent *frittura all'italiana*.

€ **Gastronomia L.u.i.s.e**, via Santa Caterina a Chiaia 68, **T** 081-417735. *Mon-Sat 0800-2030, Sun 0930-1430.* *Map 4, J8, p253* Right on piazza dei Martiri this is good for Neapolitan fast food: savoury pastries, fritture, pre-cooked pasta etc. Pick and choose from a counter and eat in or take-away.

Cafés and pasticcerie

Casa Ferrieri, via Filangieri 75, **T** 081-405221. *Mon-Sat 0700-2200, Sun 0700-2300. Near piazza dei Martiri.* *Map 4, I8, p253* An exceptionally good selection of cakes, available by the slice, as well as a wide range of delicious pastries. Their coffee is excellent too.

Gelaterie

Chiquitos, via Mergellina. *In front of the Funicolare, no phone.* Chiquitos is one of the chalets opposite Mergellina Port and as such you might not expect much from it. Actually, however, it sells great ice-cream, and has an impressive range. Specialities include Mars and Profiterol, the latter for those who like their chocolate ice-cream to be properly chocolatey. *Chalet Ciro* nearby is also excellent, but its reputation means long queues.

Vomero

Restaurants

€€ **Acunzo**, via D Cimarosa 64, **T** 081-5785362. *Mon-Sat 1300-1500, 1930-2330*. *Map 4, C2, p252* Serving pizzas alongside traditional Neapolitan fare, this is a decent spot for a quick bite of lunch on your way to the Certosa San Martino. Apparently Jack Lemmon and Marcello Lippi have both done so before.

€€ **Trattoria Vanvitelli**, piazza Vanvitelli 9c, **T** 081-5563015. *Mon-Sun 1200-1530, 1800-0100*. *Map 4, B2, p252* Despite its pleasant tree-lined courtyard at the back, this restaurant is a bit too big to have much character. The fixed-price 3-course menu is good, however, and at €7.75, very good value. They also double as a pizzeria.

€ **Osteria Donna Teresa**, via Kerbaker 58, **T** 081-5567070. *Mon-Sat 1200-1500, 1800-2300*. *Map 4, C3, p252* This small, plain restaurant has a limited choice but good, solid Neapolitan food. A pasta dish (usually from a choice of two), a main course and a drink will cost you €9 and you'll leave feeling very full. It can feel a little hurried though, and without any Italian you might struggle.

Gelaterie

Soave, via Scarlatti 130, **T** 081-5567411. *Mon-Sat 0800-1330, 1630-1900*. *Map 4, B3, p252* Soave also sells cheeses from a room at the back but most come for its ice-creams, which are excellent.

Otranto, via Scarlatti 78, **T** 081-5587498. *0930-2300, closed Wed*. *Map 4, C1, p252* Some of Naples' most exquisite ice-cream can be found here in the heart of Vomero's passeggiata territory. There also do very good ice-cream-filled cakes and pastries.

Pozzuoli

Restaurants

€€ **La Cucina**, largo San Paolo 19, **T** 081-5269060. *1230-1530, 2000-0000, closed Tue.* One of Pozzuoli's best-known restaurants, in a good position right by the port.

€€ **Don Antonio**, via Magazzini 20, **T** 081-5267941. *Mon-Sun 1230-1500, 1900-0000.* Downmarket but delicious, this is an excellent trattoria serving good and very cheap traditional dishes.

€ **Da Ciuffello**, via Dicearchia 11, **T** 081-5269397. *Mon-Sun 1200-1530, 2000-0100.* Pozzuoli is well-known for its seafood. *Trattoria Da Ciuffello*, between the Cumana station and the port, is a good place to try the local fish soup, and has some outside tables.

Sorrento

Restaurants

€€ **Trattoria il Buco**, il rampa Marina Piccola 5, **T** 081-8782354. *1200-1430, 1900-2330, closed Wed. Just off piazza San Antonio, down some steps under an arch.* This is maybe as near as you'll get in Sorrento to a traditional trattoria. Built into the Porto Marinella, one of the ancient gates of the town (c700AD), service can be less than attentive but the food is good.

€€ **San Antonio**, via Santa Maria delle Grazie 6, **T** 081-8771200. *1100-1530, 1900-0000 or later.* With a pleasant raised terrace complete with orange trees, good pizzas and a reasonable range of other traditional regional dishes at relatively good prices, this is one of Sorrento's better restaurant options, well-used by locals as well as tourists.

€€ **La Lanterna**, via Cesareo 23-25, **T** 081-8781355. *1200-1500, 1900-0000, closed Wed.* A line of small tables outside on the narrow street are the most desirable places to eat in this decent pizzeria/restaurant. It must be doing something right, since two other branches are now open around town.

Gelaterie

Bougainvillea, corso Italia 16, **T** 081-8781364. *0830-0000, closed Mon winter. Bougainvillea* is an overwhelming place. It claims to have "over 72 different flavours" but on a good day you might count a hundred. It's very hard to find one that isn't absolutely delicious. They even do slim-line ice-cream, sugar-free and low in fat. Remember, though, that you're supposed to be on holiday.

Capri

Restaurants

€€€ **Aurora**, via Fuorlovado 18-22, **T** 081-8370181. *1200-1500, 1900-0000, closed Nov-Easter except one week over New Year.* Possibly Capri's best eatery, Aurora has been in the D'Alessio family for three generations. The place is elegant, there are 300 wines to choose from, service is excellent and portions are reassuringly tiny.

€€ **Mamma Giovanna**, via Boffe 3/5, **T** 081-8372057. *1145-1500, 1900-2330, closed Wed Sep-Jun.* On the quiet and picturesque piazza A Diaz, this excellent little restaurant does a good line in Pennette Aumm Aumm (with tomatoes and aubergines) and *Orecchiette Boscaiolo* (with mushrooms) as well as some good fried fish.

€€ **Verginiello**, via lo Palazzo 25, **T** 081-8370944. *1200-1500, 1930-0000. Just down the hill from via Roma.* This is one of Capri's best pizzerias, though they also do a reasonable traditional menu. There is a quiet terrace overlooking Marina Grande and the sea.

€ **Add'o Riccio**, via Grotta Azzurra 11, **T** 081-8371380. *Mon-Sun 1200-1600, Sat-Sun 2000-0000. Out of Anacapri town towards the Grotta Azzurra.* This friendly restaurant is worth the extra distance for its enormous portions of delicious seafood spaghetti.

€ **Buca di Bacco "da Serafina"**, via Longano 25, Capri Town **T** 081-8370723. *1200-1500, 1900-0000, closed Wed.* Not far from the piazzetta, this little restaurant is about as close as Capri gets to a traditional trattoria. The food is good, fresh and cheap and the clientele as local as it ever gets around here.

€ **Moscardino**, via Roma 28, **T** 081-8370687. *1200-1500, 1930-2200.* Better than you might imagine from its position (near the bus stop) and its exterior, the friendly Moscardino has a menu which changes, always a good sign, and a good selection of pasta and seafood dishes. The 'Light Lunch' menu is also worth a look.

Ischia

Restaurants

€€ **Ristorante Coco**, via Aragonese 1, Ischia Ponte, **T** 081-981823. *Mon-Sun 1230-1530, 1930-0000.* Given its position, almost on the 'bridge', directly opposite the castle, this ought to be an expensive tourist trap. However, for now at least it is an excellent, if slightly brusque, and decently priced restaurant with a mainly Italian clientele. The simple pasta and fish are especially recommended.

€€ **Da Pasquale**, via Sant'Angelo 79, **T** 081-904208. *1230-1500, 1900-0000, closed Tue Oct-Apr. Set back from the seafront in Sant'Angelo up a quiet street.* A busy and loud pizzeria with a mostly Italian crowd. Its pizzas are excellent.

€€ **Mamma Mia**, via Sant'Angelo 62, **T** 081-999273. *Mon-Sun 1200-1500, 1900-2200. Above Sant'Angelo, overlooking the beaches of Maronti, this popular restaurant has an excellent fish menu.* The supermarket music and the caricatures of the moustachioed owner may not be everyone's cup of tea but the food is fresh and expertly cooked. You may be offered a delicious basil liqueur as a digestivo.

€ **Snack Bar La Siesta**, via F Buonocore 36, Ischia Porto, **T** 081-991307. *Mon-Sun 0900-0000. Just back from the public beach in Ischia Porto.* Abundantly flowery and relaxed, this place does excellent panini and large salads. Also a good place for a drink.

€ **Al Pontile**, via L Mazzella 15, Ischia Ponte, **T** 081-983492. *1000-0200 every day, except Wed Nov-Mar. In an excellent position just back from the castle.* Al Pontile describes itself as a bar-paninoteca, though its range of light meals and snacks are worth coming here for as well. It's also a very hospitable place and almost always open.

Cafés

Bar Il Grottino, via Roma 22, Ischia Porto, **T** 081-991591. *0730-0200.* Probably the best coffee in Ischia Porto is served here, in probably its most Italian bar. Excellent cornetti too.

Gelaterie

Bar di Maoi, piazza Antica Reggia, Ischia Porto, **T** 081-991870. *0730-0000 or later.* At the southeast corner of Ischia's port this gelateria sells very good ice-cream and is almost always busy.

Procida

Restaurants

€€ **Ristorante la Conchiglia**, via Pizzaco 10, Procida,
T 081-8967602. *1330-1600 Apr-Nov, 2030-2300 May-Oct. Down on the beach at Spiaggia Chiaia.* La Conchiglia does some exceptionally good food in a lovely setting. The house special of pasta with green beans, sun-dried tomatoes and cheese is mouth-wateringly good, salads are abundant and the seafood is excellent and predictably fresh. After a swim it all tastes even better.

€€ **Osteria del Gallo**, 82 via Roma, Marina Grande,
T 081-8101919. *1030-late afternoon, 1900-late evening, closed Thu Dec and Jan.* At this popular place along the seafront the fish dishes are fairly standard but the pasta is excellent and the atmosphere genial. €16 for two courses plus wine.

€ **La Piazzetta**, piazza dei Martiri, Corricella, **T** 081-8967245. Really more of a take-away joint, the Piazzetta does a mean pizza, and when it's warm enough to be outside the location is also excellent. If it isn't, however, you may have to put up with a blaring TV.

Cafés

Bar Capriccio, via Roma 99, Marina Grande, **T** 081-8969506.
0700-0130 or later, closed Thu in winter. Only a very short walk from the ferry. The right place to get your bearings over a morning pastry and coffee. Later it becomes more lively and is an affable place for an evening drink.

Positano

Restaurants

€€ **Buca di Bacco**, via Rampa Teglia 8, **T** 089-811461.
0830-0200 (0300 Sat). Buca di Bacco, just back from the beach, is
a café but also a restaurant (confusingly called *'La Pergola'*). It is
especially good for coffee and pastries. Food is generally expensive
but there are big salads which are better value.

€€ **La Cambusa**, piazza Vespucci 4, **T** 089-875432. *1200-1530,
1900-2330.* Probably the best of the restaurants directly behind the
beach, *La Cambusa* has a useful, visual fish translation menu.

€€ **O'Guarracino**, via Posianesi d'America 12, **T** 089-875794.
1200-1500, 1930-0000. West of the port. With views over Spiaggia
Fornillo, *O' Guarracino* does an excellent selection of traditional
dishes. The *linguine zucchine* and *linguine Guarracino* (mixed seafood) are both good.

€ **O'Capurale**, via Regina Giovanna 12, **T** 089-811188. *1230-1500,
1900-2300. Back from the west end of the beach. O'Capurale's* monolin-
gual menu is a sign that, almost uniquely, it isn't completely a slave
to the tourist market. Good, big pasta dishes include *Caporalessa*: a
delicious baked dish with cheese, tomatoes and aubergines. There
are tables outside but they're on rather a slope.

Amalfi

Restaurants

€€€ **La Caravella**, via Matteo Camera 12, **T** 089-871029.
1200-1415, 1930-2230 (2200 in winter), closed Tue. A restaurant with

ambition, *La Caravella* takes the local traditions and adds a little something: its ravioli come stuffed with provola and rucola, and you can have fresh pasta with broccoli flowers, shrimps and saffron.

€€ **Da Maria**, via Lorenzo d'Amalfi 14, **T** 089-871880. *1200-1530, 1900-2330, closed Mon. Just up the street from the piazza.* Amalfi's best pizzas come from this trattoria and local dishes are also good.

€€ **San Giuseppe**, via Ruggiero 11, **T** 089-872640. *1200-1500, 1900-2330, closed Thu. Tucked away up narrow streets west of the piazza.* Decent pizzas are cooked in a wood oven and the fresh *pasta scialatielli* (a local speciality, fairly thick short strips) with seafood may be one of the best you'll taste.

€€ **Eolo**, via Pantalone Comte 3, **T** 089-871241. *1230-1430, 1930-2330, closed Tue. At the eastern end of town.* Excellent seafood and freshly baked bread can be had at this refined restaurant. You may need to book for one of the tables overlooking the town.

Gelaterie

Il Pianeta del Gelato, via Lorenzo d'Amalfi 5, **T** 089-871309. *0600-0000.* Amalfi aficionados claim this place does the world's best ice-cream. It's not cheap and the choice of flavours is limited, but it is pretty good.

Cafés and pasticcerie

La Pansa, piazza Duomo 40, **T** 089-871065. *0830-0000, closed Tue.* Still in the Pansa family after five generations and with an interior which only Gambrinus in Naples can match for faded grandeur, *La Pansa* café, right on the square, is the best place to get Amalfi's famous *Delizie al Limone*: pastries with a lemon theme.

Ravello

Restaurants

€€€ **Palazzo della Marra**, via della Marra 7, **T** 089-858302. *1200-1430, 1900-2100.* In a 12th-century villa, the *Palazzo della Marra* is authentically palatial, and has food to match, excellent local dishes with imaginative twists served under medieval arches. If the prices are off-putting there is a cheaper tourist menu.

€€ **Ristorante-Pizzeria Vittoria**, via dei Rufolo 3, **T** 089-857947. *1230-1500, 1900-2300.* Near the centre, this restaurant is smart but lacks much character. However, it does good pizzas at lunchtime and in the evening as well as a reasonable range of other dishes. Like many other restaurants in Ravello they offer a 15% reduction if you can produce concert tickets for the evening.

€€ **Cumpa' Cosimo**, via Roma 44, **T** 089-857156. *1230-1500, 1900 'until everyone goes home'.* A kind of up-market trattoria, this is very much a Ravello-style restaurant. Produce is local, seasonal and fresh and portions are generous but the dishes are slightly more refined than average, and prices are correspondingly higher.

€€ **Ristorante Garden**, via Boccaccio 4, **T** 089-857226. *1200-1500, 1900-2100.* The garden looking down a steep cliff, is a lovely place to sit on a warm evening. Both the antipasti and sea-food are good.

The line between club and bar and café (and even between bar and restaurant) is fairly blurred in Naples. There's no tradition of drinking without eating, and many *vini e cucina* (wine and cooking) places open for dinner and then stay open until the early hours. Good examples of this are *La Cantina di Albi Cocca* and *Vinarium*, both in Chiaia (see p159 and 160). There are more straightforward bars around the university though, and others are starting to spring up. The emphasis, however, is on socializing rather than raucous drinking, and much of this happens outside in the street. The scene is generally young and energetic: loud and grungy in the Centro Storico, better-dressed and more chic in Chiaia. Cafés sell alcohol and many stay open late and take on the atmosphere of bars. An excellent example of this is café *Intra Moenia* in piazza Bellini (see p155).

Areas which buzz until late are: around piazza Bellini and via Benedetto Croce in the Centro Storico; borgo Marinari, by the Castel dell'Ovo; Chiaia, mainly to the west of piazza dei Martiri; and Mergellina. Many places do not get busy until after midnight.

Most of the city's big **clubs** are out of town, particularly in Pozzuoli, and are hard to get to and from without a car. Many of the city centre's clubs are small affairs where you may be required to become a member (you will probably be asked for a *tessera* at the door, this is a membership card). This is a way of getting around licensing requirements and will rarely be expensive (and occasionally free).

Nothing gets going much before midnight, though places generally open around 2200 or 2300. Closing times vary from place to place and from night to night but are rarely before 0300. Many clubs move to the beach in summer – check the local press for details.

Cafés thankfully usually open early enough for a well-earned sfogliatella and cappuccino at the end of the night.

Bars

Naples

Kinky Bar, via Cisterna dell'Olio 21, **T** 081-5521571. *Free. Map 2, E1, p248* Specializing in reggae and dub, *Kinky Bar* has a dance floor but mostly people here are too chilled out to use it.

Vibes Bar, largo San Giovanni Maggiore 26/27, **T** 081-5513984. *Mon-Fri 2000-0300, Sat-Sun 1900-0300. Map 2, F4, p248* Lively *Vibes Bar* spills out into a quiet piazza near the university for most of the year and even in winter there never seem to be enough chairs. The atmosphere is loud and informal rather than sophisticated.

Tempio di Bacco, vico San Domenico Maggiore 1, **T** 081-294354. *Map 2, F4, p248* This atmospheric wine bar is in old cellars just north of piazza San Domenico Maggiore. Blue lights, chains holding up tables, fish tanks, silver bunches of grapes and laid-back jazzy grooves all contribute to a distinctly chilled atmosphere. Wonderfully eclectic collection of glasses and good snacks.

Le Bar, via Eldorado 7, piazzetta Marinari 18, borgo Marinari, **T** 081-7645722. *Map 3, L4, p251* Slightly more streetwise than some of its neighbours in borgo Marinari, *Le Bar* attracts a fashionable 20s/30s crowd and occasionally has live music. Seats outside face the other bars and restaurants.

Transatlantico, Borgo Marinari, **T** 081-7648842. *1200-1600, 1900-0000, closed Tue. Map 3, L4, p251* With plenty of outdoor seats on both sides, *Transatlantico* is a good (though pricey) place for either people- or yacht-watching. It has an up-market air, a good cocktail menu and some excellent desserts.

Be Bop Bar, via Ferrigni 34, **T** 081-2451321. *Map 4, J7, p253* While the other venues on via Ferrigni have huge crowds of young people hanging around outside busy not doing very much, this place continues to groove to its own beat in a more laid-back kind of way. A very pleasant place to come and chat over a beer.

La Focaccia Express, via Belledonne a Chiaia 31, **T** 081-412277. *Map 4, J7, p253* When you've had enough of squeezing your way to the bars of Chiaia's top nightspots, this is a great place to come and chill with a beer and a tasty slice or two of focaccia pizza, piping hot from the oven.

Clubs

Naples
See also Jazz club listings, p183.

Living Room, via Sedile di Porto 55, **T** 081-5525709. *Thu-Sun 2200-0400, membership/entrance €2. Map 2, G4, p248* This friendly place, hidden away down some stairs near the university, is indeed reminiscent of someone's living room. It's laid back, with comfy chairs and mood lighting. There are usually exhibitions of art on the walls. Music complements the atmosphere and dancing usually starts late.

Lorna Dooné, vico Satriano 10, **T** 339-2664786. *Sep-Jul Tue-Sun 1900-0330. Free entrance.* Usually too packed to be able to do much breathing, let alone dancing, this is nevertheless a top spot at which to be seen.

Velvet, via Cisterna dell Olio 11, **T** 347-8661289. *Map 2, E1, p248* A funky if eclectic mix of reggae, jazz, house, garage and trip-hop plays to a trendy young crowd in this popular club. There is also occasional live music.

Echos, vico San Geronimo, **T** 081-292372. *Entrance cost and times vary. Map 2, E4, p248* A good mix of interesting live acts and up-for-it nights with DJs. Music ranges from ska to rock to tango as well as themed tribute nights to well-known stars.

Notting Hill, piazza Dante 88A, **T** 081-5540839. *2230-0500, closed Mon. Free entrance but drink obligatory. Map 2, D1, p248* A homage to all things vaguely indie, especially those with a London feel, this dark place also has a good reputation for live acts which play two or three times a week.

My Way, via Cappella Vecchia 30, **T** 081-2451887. *Map 3, J1, p251* Carved out of the rock near piazza dei Martiri, *My Way* has an energetic young crowd who dance to a disco beat.

S'move, vico dei Sospiri 10a, **T** 081-7645813. *0800-0500. Map 4, J7, p253* In *S'move*'s daily evolution from bar to club, a DJ and 'music lounge' take over from 1800 with the predominantly house 'discobar' from 2200.

Amalfi Coast and Sorrento

Away from the city, other locations around the bay tend to have a limited nightlife. The islands have little other than café-bars, though many of these do stay open late. Sorrento's cafés are supplemented by various English/Irish bars, none of which can be especially recommended. The Amalfi Coast fares slightly better, but only just.

Africana, via Torre a Mare 2, Praiano **T** 089-874042. *Mon-Sun Jun-Sep closed Oct-May*. The Amalfi Coast's most famous club is accessible by boat transfer from both Amalfi and Positano. Set in caves above a beach the Africana has a glass-bottomed dancefloor through which you can look down on fish swimming below.

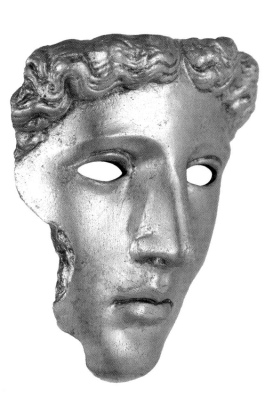

Arts and entertainment

Naples, always struggling to keep up with its past, was once a world centre for opera, theatre and popular song. Nowadays it can't quite match the heady days of Commedia dell'Arte, 17th- and 18th-century opera and *O Sole Mio*. However, since the beginning of Bassolino's 1990s arts-friendly regime, the contemporary Naples arts scene has begun to blossom. The city also does quite well out of old glories, with a prolific Baroque classical music scene, grand opera at the Teatro di San Carlo and a thriving jazz underworld.

In film, Naples is the city that gave the world of cinema Sophia Loren, Vittorio De Sica and Totò in the 1950s and 60s, though it suffered a slowdown thereafter. In recent years it has seen something of a revival, with the *Vesuviani* directors winning some major international awards.

Cinema

While Sophia Loren wowed people the world over and Totò, part Chaplin part Pulcinella, became Italy's most famous star (although he found international success harder to come by), it was Vittorio De Sica who was Naples' most influential cinematic son. Born in the city in 1901, he initially became a popular actor and singer in Fascist Italy. For *Ladri di Biciclette* (Bicycle Thieves, 1948), his neorealist masterpiece, there was pressure from Hollywood to use Cary Grant in the lead role but De Sica held firm and used a cast made up entirely of amateurs. Though much of his work was in Rome he returned to Naples in the 1960s to make some of his best films.

There have been signs of something of a revival in Neapolitan film in the last 10 years, director Mario Martone leading the way with his bleak but well-received *L'Amore Molesto* (1995) and actor and comedian Massimo Troisi posthumously becoming an international star (and receiving a Best Leading Actor Oscar nomination) for his stuttering part in *Il Postino* (1994). Troisi's roles in *Ricomincio da Tre* and *Non ci Resta che Piangere* are also well worth seeing.

Pappi Corsicato is another of Naples' *nuovi registi Vesuviani* – bright young directors trying to create a distinct Southern Italian cinematic style. He is often compared to Almodóvar, and his playful mix of camp melodrama, sensuality and existentialism do owe something to the Spanish director, though his sense of humour is very much his own. He perhaps hasn't yet bettered his debut film *Libera* (1992), though *Chimera* (2001) was also generally well-received.

Corsicato was also involved in the notorious 1996 project *I Vesuviani*, with Martone, Antonio Capuano and two other Neapolitan directors. In five parts and dealing with memory and fantasy, the film was ambitiously conceived and much criticized.

Oscar-winning Gabriele Salvatores, one of Italy's success-ful and popular directors, was born in Naples in 1950, but has tended to look elsewhere for subject matter. However, his 1993 film, *Sud*, dealt with the problems of the city of his birth and came complete with a soundtrack from Neapolitan band *99 Posse* (see p184).

Films to use Naples as a backdrop include Roberto Rossellini's *Viaggio in Italia* (1953), in which the Neapolitan landscape is used as a metaphor, Ingrid Bergman and George Sanders' marriage falling apart around the ruins of Pompeii. Others are De Sica's *Ieri, Oggi, Domani* (1963) and *Matrimonio all'Italiana* (1964), both starring Sophia Loren and Marcello Mastroianni.

In the summer, Naples' **Cinema d'Estate festival** (June-August) has films screened outdoors in monuments such as Castel Sant'Elmo and in the piazzas and parks of the city.

As in the rest of Italy, foreign films in their original language are hard to find. The *Amadeo* and *Academy Astra* cinemas both show art-house films but the Astra's are always dubbed and the Amadeo's are only occasionally in *lingua originale*. The *Abadir* has weekly showings of films in their original language in the winter but it's mainly mainstream Hollywood fare.

Cinemas

Abadir, via Paisiello, **T** 081-5789447, films most Tuesdays Oct-May in *lingua originale*.

Academy Astra, via Mezzocannone, **T** 081-5520713. *Map 2, E4, p248*.

Amadeo, via Martucci, **T** 081-680266. *Map 4, I3, p253*.

Music

Classical music and opera

A centre of Italian music for hundreds of years, Naples still has an excellent classical music culture. Other than the obvious (opera and large-scale classical concerts at the **Teatro di San Carlo**), however, you may need to scratch below the surface to find it.

Opera is the musical form that most neatly fits the Neapolitan psyche. Born out of Baroque exuberance and love of elaborate theatricality, Naples is one of its most natural homes. Neapolitan opera went through its golden period in the 17th and 18th centuries, when a dividing line was drawn between serious and comic opera. Naples excelled at the latter and became the centre of the genre. The city's most famous composer, however, Alessandro Scarlatti, was an exponent of *opera seria*, with its grandiose *da capo* arias.

The **Associazione Scarlatti** organize a good programme of chamber music in various venues, much of it in the Teatro delle Palme. There is also an excellent small local baroque scene, based around the Capella della Pietà de' Turchini. Other concerts can often be heard at the Lutheran Church, the Anglican Church and the Goethe Institute. The **Ravello Concerts** are the pick of the various music festivals and seasons in the area, both for quality and setting (see below and p117).

Associazione Alessandro Scarlatti, piazza dei Martiri 58, **T** 081-406011, www.napoli.com/assocscarlatti *Map 4, K8, p253* Concerts from about €15 upwards.

Cappella della Pietà de' Turchini, via Santa Caterina da Siena 38, **T** 081-402395, www.turchini.it *Map 3, D1, p250* Tickets from about €5. The Baroque Orchestra Cappella della Pietà de' Turchini hold excellent regular concerts of mainly Neapolitan music in the attractive Chiesa di Santa Caterina da Siena.

Chiesa Anglicana (Christ Church), via San Pasquale a Chiaia 15b, **T** 081-411842, murrayg@libero.it *Map 4, J5, p253*

Chiesa Evangelica Luterana, via Carlo Poerio 5, **T** 081-663207, www.lutero.org *Map 4, K8, p253*

Goethe Institute, riviera di Chiaia 202, **T** 081-411923, www.goethe.de/napoli *Map 4, K5, p253* An interesting programme of events with a Germanic theme can be seen for free at the Goethe Institute. Evenings often consist of film together with live music.

Teatro delle Palme, via Vetriera 12, **T** 081-418134. *Map 3, H6, p251*

Teatro di San Carlo, tickets: via San Carlo 98f, **T** 081-7972331, www.teatrosancarlo.it *Tue-Sat 1000-1300, 1630-1830, Sun 1000-1300. Map 3, E5, p250* The San Carlo is one of the most prestigious opera houses in Italy, and the standard of concerts and opera here is world-class if seldom mould-breaking. Audiences tend to be demanding but steadfastly traditional. Capable of seating over 1,000 people, it is also one of the biggest. The acoustics are also famously good, and the interior is breathtakingly grand. Prices vary depending on the music, but start at around €20, €26 for opera.

An excellent selection of classical concerts is held in the **Villa Rufolo** in Ravello. These are particularly popular in the summer when they are held outdoors in the gardens with the spectacular backdrop of the Amalfi Coast. See p117 for details.

Neapolitan song

Naples' most famous era as a source of popular song was the first few decades of the 20th century. While the stereotype singing of *O Sole Mio* on street corners may be hard to track down, you'll probably hear it, and *Funicolì Funicolà*, or at least their descendants, in many bars, cafés and restaurants around the city. The origins of these sentimental but heartfelt outpourings lie partly in Neapolitan opera, but also in a long history of popular song going back to the 16th century. A degree of irony in the original classics was lost in *sceneggiata*, a theatre genre which followed them, and is also hard to discern in the many modern spin-offs.

Napoli nella Raccolta de Mura (Napoli in the De Mura Collection), piazza Trieste e Trento. *Mon-Sat 0900-1900, Sun 0900-1300. Free. Map 3, F4, p250* Programmes, posters, pictures and memorabilia from the golden age of Neapolitan song. See p40.

Jazz

A good jazz scene revolves mostly around the *Otto Jazz Club* where you may find impromptu music from the groups of local musicians who gather there as well as an excellent advertised programme.

Otto Jazz Club, piazzetta Cariati 24, **T** 081-666262. *Thu-Sun. Map 3, C1, p250* One of Italy's most respected jazz clubs plays host to live local, national and international jazz. A bar also serves snacks.

Murat, via V. Bellini 8, **T** 081-5445919/3480348822, muratliveclub@tiscali.it *Wed-Sun 1900-0200. Map 2, C1, p248* Hand-painted tables, panini and expertly-mixed cocktails all add to the atmosphere in this jazz-orientated club. Live music usually starts at 2200.

Contemporary

Much of Naples' more interesting contemporary music over the last 10 to 15 years has been born from the left-wing, often illegally occupied *centri sociali* (social centres), in particular **Officina 99**, via Gianturco 101, **T** 081-7349091, www.officina99.org, from which rap group **99 Posse** were born. Much of their music is associated with marginalized youth and the disaffected and is sung in dialect. 99 Posse are now rich pop stars but still sing and rap in dialect, and remain political.

Almamegretta, www.almamegretta.net, is another political Neapolitan band whose mixing of musical roots from Campania with reggae, dub, funk and African musical traditions has brought them national success. They continue to explore serious issues, particularly the political and economic exploitation of the south, and have worked with Massive Attack. Their 2001 album *Immaginaria* was critically acclaimed.

Pino Danielle came from a similar background, starting as a protest singer for Neapolitan workers, but he has now become mellow and rather dull (and a national superstar) and sings in Italian as opposed to dialect.

The other strong thread running through local contemporary music is that of the **Nuovi Melodici**. Originating in the Quartieri Spagnoli, the music of the various artists classed as the Nuovi Melodici is also sung in dialect but is much more conservative, both musically and thematically.

Venues for contemporary music in the city are generally small-scale, such as *Notting Hill* (p175) and *Vibes Bar* (p173), though large-scale concerts such as Festivalbar (in piazza del Plebiscito, see p190) and Neapolis (currently in the Parco Virgiliano, see p190) are becoming more of a feature.

Theatre

Naples' most famous theatrical export is **Commedia dell'Arte**, a stylized form of theatre from the 16th century which elevated jugglers, clowns and stock characters such as Harlequin and, in Naples' case, Pulcinella from entertainers into stars. Pulcinella is one of the city's symbols: a white cloaked man with a black mask and a long nose, he is seen as the personification of the Neapolitan character. Passionate yet lazy, he overindulges and is, in turn, despondent and exuberant. He breaks the law and beats the local policeman with a stick. His wife, exasperated, does the same to him. If this sounds at all familiar it is probably because he is also the source of Punch, of Punch and Judy fame. His descendants can be seen playing the banjo in piazza del Plebiscito, or as figures for the nativity scene in via San Gregorio Armeno.

The roots of Commedia dell'Arte go back probably to the Roman *fabula Atellana*, comic theatre which also featured masked characters. Since the 16th century its influence has continued, on opera, theatre and films, notably those of Totò.

The Neapolitan theatre scene today, however, is slightly limp and conventional in comparison. There are interesting things happening, but they tend to be swamped by the largely mediocre mainstream. One notable exception to this is **Roberto de Simone**, whose successful productions are an intriguing blend of tradition, dialect and the avant-garde. These can often be seen at the Mercadante. De Simone's *La Gatta Cenerentola* ran successfully in London in 1999.

Theatres

Bellini, via Conte di Ruvo, **T** 081-5499688, www.teatrobellini.it *Map 2, B1, p248* The grand and ornate interior of the Bellini often holds large-scale musicals.

Mercadante, piazza Municipio 1, **T** 081-5513396, http://comune.napoli.it/mercada.htm *Map 3, C6/7, p250* One of the city's most interesting theatres, often home to Roberto de Simone (see above) as well as actor and director Luca de Filippo (www.defilippo.it), another bright star of southern Italian theatre.

Sancarluccio, via S Pasquale 49, **T** 081-405000. *Map 4, H5, p253* Foreign imports and some more experimental work.

Sannazaro, via Chiaia 157, **T** 081-411723, www.teatrosannazaro.it *Map 3, F1, p250* A beautiful old theatre often filled with TV actors doing comedy.

Festivals and events

Naples' calendar of special events is dominated by Maggio dei Monumenti, when hundreds of talks, tours, concerts and exhibitions take place around the city, often in buildings that are closed for the rest of the year. The less well-publicized Settimana per la Cultura, in April, is also a good time for visiting monuments and museums, as hours are extended and most are free. Religious festivals are good for less tourist-orientated celebrations: Natale (Christmas) has nativity scene fever in via San Gregorio Armeno accompanied by concerts and other events and Pasqua (Easter) has colourful processions in Naples and all around the area. For a party try Capodanno (New Year) in piazza del Plebiscito or the July Neapolis Rock Festival. Outside the city in the summer discos often escape to the beaches and classical musicians take up position in dramatic outdoor settings such as the Villa Rufolo in Ravello.

Dates of events often vary from year to year. Where specific dates are not listed here, check with tourist information.

January

Capodanno (New Year): big concert (night of 31st Dec) and fireworks in piazza del Plebiscito.

March

Benvenuto Primavera: tours of, and events in, Naples' gardens, **T** 081-2471123. **Chamber Music on the Amalfi Coast**: (Mar-Nov) Ravello and around. Ravello Concert Society, **T** 089-858149, **F** 089-858249, www.ravelloarts.org Book in advance for these increasingly high-profile concerts (tickets €20) which in high season are given outdoors in the gardens of Villa Rufolo (p117) with the spectacular backdrop of the Amalfi Coast behind and below. **Maratona Città di Napoli**: Naples' marathon finishes in piazza del Plebiscito. **Easter: Pasqua a Napoli**, concerts in Naples' churches; **Good Friday**; processions all over, especially on Procida and in Sorrento and Massa Lubrense.

April

Settimana per la Cultura: free admittance and special opening hours for a week in publicly owned museums, www.beniculturali.it **ATP Tour Challenge**: international tennis tournament, Tennis Club Napoli (see sport, p208).

May

Maggio dei Monumenti: one of the most successful initiatives of Mayor Bassolino, Maggio dei Monumenti, an idea started in 1994, is now cemented in the Neapolitan calendar. The concept is that the buildings of the city should be opened up to the public during this month. Tours are given, exhibitions are held and special events take place such as dance performances and concerts, especially at weekends. Each year there's a slightly different theme. The 'month' is stretched now, and usually starts on the last weekend in April and continues until the first in June. Much is free and it helps make May the busiest month of the year in the city. Ask at tourist information for some recommendations or check www.napoli.com for a list of events in English. **Festivalbar**: (May-Sep) televised concerts around Italy, often starting or finishing in piazza del Plebiscito. The Naples concert is free and usually attracts big international stars as well as the Italian stalwarts. The 2002 concert included The Red Hot Chilli Peppers, Alanis Morisette, Simple Minds and Sophie Ellis Bextor in its line-up. See www.festivalbar.it **Spring Primavera nel Parco**: Ufficio Promozione dell'Ente Parco Nazionale del Vesuvio, piazza Municipio 8, San Sebastiano al Vesuvio, **T** 081-7710925, www.parks.it Guided walks, visits to wine-makers and restaurants and exhibitions make up this celebration of the Parco Nazionale del Vesuvio (Vesuvius National Park).

June

Palio delle Quattro Repubbliche Marinare: boat race between Venice, Pisa, Genoa and Amalfi with lots of historical costume. Not in Amalfi until 2005. **Estate a Napoli**: (Jun-Aug) open air happenings (film, music, theatre) around the city. **St Andrea**: (Jun 27th) fireworks and processions in Amalfi.

July

Neapolis Festival: international rock festival in Parco Virgiliano which the organizers ambitiously call a 'Mediterranean Woodstock'. Tickets and information widely available from agencies (such as Box Office, Galleria Umberto I 15-16, **T** 081-5519188) and music shops (see p201). **International Piano Festival**: (Jul-Sep) Amalfi, piano recitals in the Chiostro del Paradiso every Friday, details from Tourist

Information. **Festa di Santa Anna**: (Jul 26th) Ischia, this procession of boats celebrate the island's patron saint. **Festa di San Pantaleone**: (Jul 27th) an enormous firework display celebrates the liquefaction of the blood of San Pantaleone in Ravello. **Festa delle Limone e Acciughe**: (Jul-Aug)) lemon and anchovy feast, Cetara, Amalfi Coast. **Jazz on the Bay**: Minori, Jul-Aug, open-air jazz concerts on the Amalfi Coast.

August

Musica d'Estate: (Aug-Sep) classical music concerts in Palazzo Murat, Positano. Information and tickets (€10) from Tourist

★ **Nativity scene figures on via San Gregorio Armeno**
Thousands swarm from all over Italy to via San Gregorio Armeno, a tiny street in Naples' Centro Storico to buy miniature figures for their nativity scenes. The annual buying frenzy keeps a whole industry busy all year round.

Information Positano or Palazzo Murat on the night. www.positanonline.it/ aast/musica.htm. **Ferragosto** (Feast of the Assumption, Aug 15th) celebrated everywhere with water fights and in some places with processions (eg Positano) or concerts (eg Naples).

September

Napoli Strit Festival: international festival of street art. **Pizza Fest**: celebration in Naples of everything that is good about the sacred round things. **Dance Festival**: Positano, 1st Fri and Sat of the month. *Li Galli d'Oro* prize for young dancers and *Leonide Massine* prize for dance. **Festa della Madonna di Piedigrotta**: (Sep 7th) what was once a high-profile song festival has become rather low-key but may be revived. **Festa di San Gennaro**: (Sep 19th) chaos and celebrations/hysteria (depending on the result) accompany the liquefaction (or not) of St Gennaro's blood in his chapel in the Duomo (see p51).

October

Incontri Internazionale del Cinema: a Sorrento film festival which concentrates on TV-films and animation. **Festival del Corto Metraggio**, international short film festival in Positano. **Maratona della Pace**: marathon from Naples to Pompeii.

December

Natale a Napoli: concerts of sacred music in churches, theatre, exhibitions and various events revolving around nativity scenes and via San Gregorio Armeno.

For a list of public holidays, see p222.

Shopping

Naples and its surrounding area offer no shortage of possibilities for souvenir-buying. Specialities include the liqueur Limoncello, stationery, ceramics and mozzarella, and at Christmas people come from all over Italy to buy figures and props for Nativity scenes from via San Gregorio Armeno in the Centro Storico.

In Naples, the largely pedestrianized via Toledo is probably the main shopping street, though Vomero is also an important commercial area. At the pedestrianized end (near piazza Trieste e Trento) via Toledo takes on a carnival air at busy times, particularly Saturday mornings, live bands and clowns entertaining the wandering crowds. Slightly smarter shops can be found along via Chaia and into piazza dei Martiri. The area around via dei Tribunali and Spaccanapoli has plenty of smaller, family-owned shops, selling everything from pasta and paper cups to entire altarpieces. Via San Sebastiano has workshops and shops making and selling musical instruments. Via Pignasecca and the Montesanto area have lots of places selling good, cheap food and household goods, as well as an excellent market.

Most shops close for siesta between about 1300 and 1600. Many food shops close on Thursday afternoons.

Antiques (see also Markets)

Madamaluna, via G Verdi 4, **T** 081-401990, www.madamaluna.it *Map 3, D5, p250* Near the Galleria, this shop sells an interesting mixture of antiques and "colonial" items.

Books

Feltrinelli, via Santa Caterina a Chiaia 23 (piazza dei Martiri), **T** 081-2405411. *Nov-May Mon-Sat 1000-2200, Sun 1000-1400, 1600-2000; Jun-Oct Mon-Sat 1000-2300, Sun 1000-1400, 1600-2100. Map 3, G1, p250* An enormous shop on the corner of piazza dei Martiri, with an excellent selection of books on several floors, this Neapolitan stalwart also has one of the cities biggest stocks of CDs, videos and DVDs. There's a café, magazines, and stationery too. The English-language section is very good.

Libreria Fiorentina, calata Trinità Maggiore 36, **T** 081-5522005, libreriafiorentina@virgilio.it *Mon-Fri 0800-1400, 1530-2000 Sat-Sun 0800-1400, but "if it's a nice sunny day I make a holiday". Map 2, F1, p248* This excellent shop sells a selection of books and prints, old and new. There is an great selection of books about Naples, though mostly in Italian, including photography, history and walks. The prints are slightly eclectic, but more interesting than the naff selection found in many shops in the Centro Storico.

Evaluna, piazza Bellini 72, **T** 081-292372, www.evaluna.it *Map 2, C2, p248* A cultural association as well as a women's bookshop, *Evaluna* has regular exhibitions, live music and poetry readings. It also becomes a 'meeting café' every evening from 2200.

Cameos

De Paola Cameos, via A Caccavello 67, **T** 0815782910. *Mon-Sat 0900-2000, Sun 0900-1200. Map 4, B6, p252* The *De Paola Cameo Factory*, near Castel Sant'Elmo, has an impressive range of cameos in various shapes and sizes. If you work for NATO you're entitled to a special discount.

Ceramics

Lisa Weber Laboratorio di Ceramica, via Paladino 4, **T** 081-457621. *Mon-Sat 1000-1330, 1700-2000. Map 2, D4, p248* Lisa Weber has a little workshop and shop just off piazzetta Nilo, making and selling a nice line in pots, cups and teapots with a handmade feel.

La Ceramica, via Roma 42, Ischia Porto, **T** 081-982699. *Mon-Sun, 0900-1300, 1600-2030.* Probably the biggest of the many ceramics shops in Ischia selling a similar range of mostly majolica-style pottery. Though much of it is a bit quaint, the range is enormous, and the jugs and limoncello cups would make good souvenirs.

Sepe, via P R Giuliani 19, Sorrento, **T** 081-8072848 www.sepeartglass.com *0930-1330, 1600-2030.* Sorrento has no shortage of ceramics shops, most selling a very similar range. This one has an above-average selection and also sells glassware.

Chocolate

Dolce Idea, via Solitaria 7/8, **T** 081-7642832; via Bonito 21B, **T** 081-5560563; via S Liborio 2, (piazza Carità), **T** 081-4203090. *Mon-Sat 0900-1430, 1530-2000, Sun 0900-1430. Map 3, G/H3, p251* Dolce Idea, with three branches around the city, make supremely good chocolate, which has won several international awards "for its seriousness and its goodness" (if you ask, they'll probably give you a well-produced booklet in Italian and English, telling you all about themselves, as well as the history of the brown stuff). Look out too for chocolate sculptures in their windows, such as a 3-dimensional model of the entire Bay of Naples.

Gay Odin, via Toledo 214, **T** 081-5513491. *Mon-Sat 0930-1330, 1630-2000. Map 3, C4, p250* Also various other locations around the city, www.gay-odin.it *Gay Odin* (named after its founder Isidore Odin and his assistant Onorina Gay, with whom he fell in love) sells a similar range of excellent chocolate, including a delicious variety made with chillies, and models of Vesuvius, attractively boxed.

Coffee

Caffè Mexico, piazza Dante 86, **T** 081-5499330. *Mon-Sat 0730-2030. Map 2, D1, p248* An excellent café (see also p158) selling a good selection of beans, all roasted on the premises.

Department stores

Coin, *Upim* and *Rinascente* all stock a selection of fashion and household (mainly kitchen) goods. While none is very inspiring they're all quite good for typical Italian fare such as espresso cups, perfume and furnishings, all with a certain Italian style. *Upim* is probably the cheapest, while *Rinascente* aspires to catering for a slightly more up-market crowd.

Coin, via Scarlatti 88/100, Vomero, **T** 081-5780111. *Mon 1620-2000, Tue-Sat 1000-1345, 1620-2000. Map 4, C2, p252*

Rinascente, via Toledo 343, **T** 081-411511. *Mon-Sat 0900-2000, Sun 1000-1400, 1700-2000.*

Upim, via Nisco 11, Chiaia, **T** 081-417520. *Mon-Sat 0930-1330, 1600-2000, Sun 1000-1330, 1630-2000.* Map 4, I6, p253

Doll Repairs

Ospedale delle Bambole, via San Luigi dei Librai 81, www.ospedaledellebambole.it *1030-1400, 1700-2000, closed Sat pm.* Map 2, C7, p249 Though it's possible that while in Naples you won't have too many urgent doll-repairs that need attending to, the Neapolitan institution of the *Ospedale delle Bambole* is well worth a visit. The little shop is stacked high with old dolls, and old bits of dolls. If you do need to check your doll in for treatment it costs €57 for 'Doll Big' and €41 for 'Doll Small'.

Food

Good delicatessens and excellent fruit and vegetables are every-where in and around Naples.

Tropical Fruits, via Montesanto 6, **T** 081-5801006. *Mon-Sat 0800-1400, 1600-2000.* Map 2, F1, p248 A sort of international healthfood shop with a difference, *Tropical Fruits* sells everything from Chinese beer to hummous to tomato ketchup and just about everything imaginable in between, including some Italian delicacies.

Two shops right next to each other on via B Croce both have an extraordinary selection of flavoured and shaped pastas, many of which hang outside the shops, completely covering the walls. They also have a good variety of olive oils, limoncello and other high-quality local produce.

    Salumeria, via B Croce 43, **T** 081-5516981. *Mon-Sat 0830-2030, Sun 0830-1400.* Map 2, E3, p248 **Fantasia Napoletana**, via B Croce, 44, **T** 081-5517081, fantasianapoletana@libero.it *Mon-Sat 0900-0830, Sun 0900-1400.* Map 2, E3, p248

La Bottega della Pasta, vico D'Afflitto 41, **T** 081-410006. *Tue-Sat 0930-1400, 1600-2000, Sun 0930-1400, closed Mon. Map 3, C3, p250* For a truly authentic fresh pasta *La Bottega della Pasta* is hard to beat. A delicious range of produce is made adjacent to the shop and sold by weight. It should keep until you get home.

Gifts and handicrafts

Riciclo, via B Croce 54, **T** 081-5529158. *Mon-Sat 1000-1400, 1630-2000, Sun 1000-1400. Map 2, E3, p248* An interesting mix of stationery, toys, lamps and various other things made from recycled paper. They also run courses in various crafts.

Kitchen

Spina, via Pignasecca 62, **T** 081-5524818. *Mon 1000-1400, Tue-Sat 1000-1400, 1600-2000, closed Sun.* This little shop in the Quartieri Spagnoli is piled high with an enormous selection of different pasta machines, corkscrews, coffee machines etc.

Limoncello

You'll find Limoncello just about anywhere, especially Sorrento, where various shops vying for trade will try and entice you in with free samples.

Limoné, piazza San Gaetano 72, **T/F** 081-299429. *Mon-Sun 1000-1400, 1600-2000, 1000-2000 in summer. Map 2, B5, p248* Just next to *Napoli Sotterranea*, *Limoné* make good-quality organic limoncello right here on the premises. They use traditional methods, and peel all their lemons by hand. They also make a variety of other lemon-related products. Ask and they'll show you the whole process. Ask nicely and they'll probably give you a taste.

> ### Limoncello recipe

Some Italian recipes for this traditional *digestivo* use 'pure' alcohol, but vodka is easier to obtain, and the end result is pretty much the same.

10 lemons, thick-skinned and preferably unwaxed
1 litre vodka
750 grammes white sugar
2 litres water

Wash the lemons well, especially if they are waxed (in which case scrub in hot water). Peel the lemons using a vegetable peeler, avoiding the white pith. Place all the peel in a large airtight jar or bottle. Pour in the vodka. Leave in a cool, dark place to infuse for a week. The vodka should turn yellow. Mix together the sugar and water in a pan and bring to the boil. Boil for 10 minutes without stirring. Leave to cool to room temperature (about 10 minutes). Strain the infused vodka into the cooled syrup. Pour the resulting mixture into glass bottles and seal. Store at room temperature (it will improve with age) but serve ice-cold from the freezer.

Fattoria Terranova, piazza Tasso 16, Sorrento, **T** 081-8781263, www.massalubrense.it/fatterranova.htm *0930-1300, 1630-2130.* In a corner of Sorrento's main square, the little shop of *Fattoria Terranova* could easily be missed. Don't though: it has an exceptional range of locally produced liqueurs and jams, from the standard limoncello to a surprisingly delicious one made with rucola (rocket). Everything is from an *agriturismo* in nearby Santa Agata sui due Golfi.

Markets

The sprawling drama that is the **Mercato di Porta Nolana** is hard to beat (see p63). *Map 2, C12, p249* A slightly less eclectic combination (mainly food) can be found every morning at **La**

Pignasecca, on and around via Pignasecca, off via Toledo. The daily **Mercato dei Fiori** (flower market) takes place at dawn on the east side of Castel Nuovo. *Map 3, p250D/E7* It's likely to be over before you've finished breakfast so make a big effort. Naples' antiques market, **Fiera Antiquaria Napoletana**, usually takes place on the last two Saturdays of the month in the Villa Comunale in Chiaia, 0800-1400, though it's less frequent in summer. *Map 4, L6, p253* Check at Tourist Information or **T** 081-621951 for dates.

Music

Sound Check, via B Croce 5, **T** 081-5516940, musique@tin.it, www.soundcheck-musique.com *Mon-Fri 1000-1400, 1500-1930, Sat 1000-1330, 1615-1930. Map 2, E2, p248* In the heart of the Centro Storico this is an excellent music shop, with various different specialties, from Rock to Fusion to Hip Hop, and a good vinyl section upstairs. It's also a good place to buy tickets to upcoming concerts, or just to find out what's happening around the city.

Perfume, toiletries and herbal medicine

Officina Profumo Farmaceutica di Santa Maria Novella, via Santa Caterina a Chiaia 20, **T** 081-407176. *Mon 1630-2015, Tue-Sat 1000-1315, 1630-2015. Map 3, G1, p251* The Neapolitan branch of this 800-year-old business is on piazza dei Martiri, and just opening the door is a truly fragrant experience. From herbal medicines that cure "almost everything" to toothpaste, to Russian Cologne soap for men, to a wide range of perfumes and aftershaves, this shop has it all. Everything is made from natural ingredients and nothing is tested on animals. If you ask they'll give you a sheet detailing the history of the company from its founding by Dominican Fathers in 1221 to the present day. This too will smell overpoweringly floral.

Shoes

With good-quality leather goods being made in abundance in and around the city there is no shortage of good shoe shops. The best areas to try are via Chiaia (smart) and via Pignasecca (good value).

Tiles

La Riggiola Napoletana, via Donnalbina 22, **T** 081-5518022. *Map 2, G2, p248* Sells a beautiful range of tiles, some of which are real works of art.

Toys

Equipaggiamento Circense, via Santa Chiara 17, **T** 081-5514230. *Mon-Sun 1000-1330, Mon, Wed, Fri also 1630-1900. Map 2, F3, p248* An excellent range of frisbees, kites, juggling equipment and other assorted goodies. Especially good for grown-up kids.

Wine

Enoteca Mercadante, corso Vittorio Emanuele 114, **T** 081-667293. *Mon-Sat 0900-1400, 1700-2030. Map 4, G3, p253* As well as selling good local cheeses, the two brothers running this shop have an excellent range and knowledge of Campanian wines.

Sport in Naples is dominated by football, and the fortunes of the Napoli side are followed as keenly here as in any other city on the planet. Neapolitans feel they have a lot to prove, especially over their hated northern rivals, and football is the most obvious outlet for their passionate sentiments. Despite the massive 80,000-seater Stadio San Paolo and memories of Maradona, the glory days of Napoli are proving hard to repeat – in the last few seasons they have bounced up and down between Serie A and Serie B. In 2002 they narrowly missed out on promotion back to Serie A despite large amounts of money spent on the squad. It may be some time before they're back up there fighting for the *scudetto* (championship).

Outside the city sport is dominated by the sea – most places have shacks by the waterfront renting out boats of all shapes and sizes and you can try sailing and diving courses from the islands.

Cycling

Napoli Bike, riviera di Chiaia 201, **T/F** 081-411934,
www.napolibike.com *Map 4, K6, p253* Rent mountain bikes for
the day but you'll need to be brave to ride one through the city.

Football

Stadio San Paolo, piazzale V Tecchio, **T** 081-2395623. *Metro to
Campi Flegrei.* In the World Cup in 1990 San Paolo was the venue for
the Italy versus Argentina semi-final. Argentina won 4-3 on penalties
and because of Maradona (see next page) much of Naples saw it as a
victory for the city over the rest of Italy.

League games usually take place at San Paolo every other
Sunday during the season. Entrance is by ticket only and the best
place to get them is near the stadium in Fuorigrotta from *Azzurro
Service*, via Francesco Galeota 19, **T** 081-5939445, **F** 081-5933851.

Gym

Colosseum Gym, via Timavo 43, Vomero,
www.palestracolosseum.it *Map 5, D1, p254* Smart gym with six
rooms totalling 1400 sq m of weights and exercise machines. There
are also classes daily in everything from kick-boxing to Latin dancing.

Jogging

Through the Villa Comunale and along the seafront between
Castel dell'Ovo and Mergellina are popular jogging routes.

Swimming

The sea is warm enough for swimming between April and October,
and never gets that cold even in winter. Off Naples it's not clean,

Diego Armando Maradona

In the inaugural season of Italy's Serie A (the top division of Italian football) in 1926-27, Napoli lost all but one of their games, which they drew. Sixty years later, with the help of one Diego Armando Maradona, they finally won their first *scudetto* (championship). They won it again three years later, and the UEFA cup too. No other southern Italian team has won the scudetto before or since. Now, over 10 years since Maradona left Naples, it is still hard to walk far through the city without seeing images of him. Newspaper stands still display papers from the day he left, there are murals of him painted on walls and new books about him are still being published.

When Maradona arrived from Barcelona in 1984, he was already a worldwide superstar. At the 1986 World Cup, fully ensconced in the Napoli side, he won the World Cup for Argentina, and in many ways for Naples.

There was also something in his character which endeared him to the Neapolitans. His cocky, over-confident, indulgent attitude to life, and his roots in the slums of Buenos Aires made him a Neapolitan before he arrived. Whereas in England he is vilified for his 'Hand of God' goal, in Naples they glory in his cheekiness.

Maradona has been called the 'liberator', and to inhabitants of the city he remains a potent symbol of Naples, proof of the greatness of the city and the whole of the South, of its ability to stand up to the brutish wealth of the North, and, far more than he was ever an Argentinean, he remains a Neapolitan. Outside Naples even his sad demise is linked to the city. Its culture of the availability of everything and anything for the right money, including drugs and women, helped destroy him.

In September 2001 Diego Maradona Junior was called up for the Italian under-17 squad. Neapolitans have great hopes for him.

★ Maradona mural
Long after the names of most 1980s footballers have been forgotten, Maradona's name and image are still everywhere in the city.

however. The city has two decent swimming pools, but neither have especially helpful or regular opening hours.

Piscina Collana, via Rossini 8, Vomero, **T/F** 081-5600907.

Piscina Scandone, via Giochi del Mediterraneo, Fuorigrotta, **T** 081-5702636. Olympic-size indoor-pool.

Tennis

The Naples Open tournament takes place every April at the Villa Comunale tennis club and usually attracts a few second-tier international stars. Entrance is usually free up until the quarter- or semi-final stage. The club also has courts for hire.

Tennis Club Napoli, Villa Comunale, viale Dohrn, **T** 081-7614656. *Map 5, J8, p255*

Walking

The Sorrento Peninsula offers some of the best walking opportunities in the area, though Ischia and Capri both have good routes too. See individual sections for details.

Watersports

From €55 upwards (25% discount Mon-Fri) you can rent a boat for the day, either from Marina Grande or Marina di Chiaolella, Procida. **Procida Diving Centre**, lungomare C Colombo 6, Marina di Chiaiolella, Procida, **T** 081-8968385, www.vacanzeaprocida.it Courses and excursions are organized by this centre based in Chiaiolella. **Barcheggiando**, via Roma, Marina Grande, **T** 081-8101934/3356321389 (mob).

In many ways Naples is a conservative city: the family is very strong here, as is religion. However, there is also a healthy disrespect for rules of any kind and perhaps it is because of this that there exists a surprisingly tolerant attitude towards all things gay. This is not to say that the gay scene is especially out in the open, or that the city is overflowing with gay clubs and bars (it isn't). Indeed the issue is often suppressed or ignored, and with children usually continuing to live with their parents into their mid-thirties, problems often arise. Capri is the most obvious gay destination in the area: it's homosexual roots can be traced back to Tiberius. There is also a small local scene in Naples, however, particularly around the university.

The lack of gay clubs means that the scene relies on gay nights in other venues, many of which change relatively often. For the most up-to-date information contact: ArciGay-Circolo Atinoo/ArciLesbica-Circolo Le Maree, an excellent and very helpful information centre shared by the Neapolitan gay and lesbian communities.

ArciGay-Circolo Atinoo/ArciLesbica-Circolo Le Maree, vico San Geronimo alle Monache 17-20, **T** 081-5528815, www.arcigaynapoli.homepad. com, www.arcilesbicanapoli. homepad.com, adamoeadamo@hotmail.com (*Arcigay*), lemaree@freemail.it (*ArciLesbica*). On a small road just west of via Mezzocannone in the Centro Storico. *ArciLesbica* organize film evenings, social dinners and monthly games of football. *ArciGay* organize meetings every Wed evening.

Saunas

Bar B, via G Manna 14, **T** 081287681, **F** 081-5536141, www.barb.homepad.com, davide.bar.b.@davidemail.it *Bar B* is a sauna which also doubles as a bar on Tue and Thu from 2100 and as a disco on Sat from 2200. It has a video room and a 'Mega Dark Room' as well as Turkish bath and Finnish sauna.

Blu Angel, Centro Direzionale Isola A/7 Civico 1, **T** 081-5625298. Claims to be the first men-only sauna in southern Italy. It has a Turkish bath, 2 Finnish saunas and a permanent exhibition of photographs by Baron Wilhelm Von Gloeden.

Clubs and club nights

Disco Underground, **T** 081-5527575/339-5477466, www.theangels.3000.it This group organize nights (Sun) in various different places around town.

Diva, via Giotto 10, piazza Medaglie d'Oro, Vomero, **T** 338-6175071. A hip night of clubbing with 'fashion house' and a 'sexy casino' hosted by *TheOtherSideGroup* every Saturday.

Kontatto, *Antica Birreria*, viale Kennedy, **T** 338-3071105. Weekly gay night (Thu 2100) in a pianobar in Fuorigrotta.

Freezer Stereobar, Centro Direzionale Isola G/6, **T** 339-2104142. Fashionable and modern but rather out of the way club (Fri 2300).

New Age, via Atri 36, **T** 081-295808/338-3208587. Internet access from 1700, disco and bar from 2130. Tue, Wed, Fri-Sun.

Bookshops

Mercurio, piazzetta Demetrio Salazar 8 (off piazza del Plebiscito), **T** 081-2400371, art.slab@tiscalinet.it *Mon 1530-2030, Tue-Sat 1000-1930, Sun 1000-1330. Map 3, G4, p251* Specializing in gay, lesbian and alternative literature this bookshop also has a terminal for internet access for €2 an hour.

Beaches

On Capri, **Spiaggia di via Krupp** (Marina Piccola) is the main hangout, while Grotta dell'Arsenale is a rocky beach-of-sorts at the foot of via Krupp often dotted with naked men. At times the whole island feels like a gay beach-club. **Rocce di Marechiaro** in Posillipo is probably Naples' best bet. In Sorrento the **Bagni Regina Giovanna** is a famous/infamous destination.

Hotels

Cavour (see p130), **Europeo** (see p127), **Gatto Blanco** (see p137) and **Miramare** (see p126) and are all gay-friendly.

Cruising

Piazza Garibaldi near Hotel Terminus is an established area but hardly salubrious. The **Bosco di Capodimonte** is better, and **piazza Bellini** is so civilized it's really just a 'meeting place'.

Children in Italy are either, depending on which way you look at it, appreciated (you'll hardly ever hear anyone telling kids to be quiet) or spoilt (most seem to be dressed in designer clothes and shades from the age of about three). Also, they're either given a lot of freedom (you'll see kids of 10 on mopeds) or smothered (you'll see kids of 40 still living with their mums and not being allowed out without a jacket on). Either way, it's certainly true that children here are generally cherished, and you won't have any problems taking them to restaurants, for example.

None of this has done much for child-friendly facilities in Naples, however, or attractions aimed specifically at children, of which there are very few. Museum displays are almost all badly labeled, and open spaces to play in are few and far between.

The hectic nature of Naples may seem at first to be far from ideal for children and an endless diet of churches and monuments would exhaust most people's attention span. Dig a bit deeper, however, and it still has more to interest kids than many cities.

The underground **Napoli Sotterranea** tours would be a good place to start. If that works well, the Roman remains under **San Lorenzo Maggiore** offer a variation on the same theme. The miniature worlds of the nativity scene shops on **via San Gregorio Armeno** (see p48) will fascinate many and the **aquarium** is handily placed in the middle of the city's best park.

Around the Bay, the steaming crater of **Vesuvius** should impress even the most battle-hardened. Similarly, the smelly fumaroles and boiling mud of **Solfatara** are excellent what-I-did-on-my-holidays material. **Pompeii** can be tiring, but most of the ruins can be clambered over, and the whole place is great for all sorts of games. Throw in a few charred human remains and some will be gripped. Ischia's **Castello Aragonese** is probably the pick of the area's castles and has the added benefit of having beaches nearby.

Outside the city there is a **zoo**, two **theme parks** and a good hands-on **science museum**. And a generous diet of ice-cream and pizza shouldn't go down badly either.

Naples

Acquario, Stazione Zoologica, Villa Comunale, **T** 081-5833263, p71. *Winter Tue-Sat 0900-1700, Sun 0900-1400, Summer Tue-Sat 0900-1800, Sun 1000-1800, closed Mon.* €1.50 *Map 4, K/L4, p253*

Napoli Sotterranea, piazza San Gaetano 68, **T** 081-296944, www.napolisotterranea.com, p55. *Mon-Fri 1200, 1400 and 1600, Thu also 2100, Sat-Sun 1200, 1400, 1600 and 1800,* €6.20. *Map 2, B5, p248*

Scavi di San Lorenzo Maggiore, piazza San Gaetano, **T** 081-2110860, p55. *Mon-Sat 0900-1700, Sun 1000-1330,* €4. *Map 2, B5, p248*

Kids

Outside Naples

Castello Aragonese, Ischia Ponte, p105. *Mar-Nov, Mon-Sun 0930-1 hr before sunset, €8.*

Giardino Zoologico, viale Kennedy 70, Mostra d'Oltremare, **T** 081-2395943. *Mon-Sun 0900-1700 (1900 in summer), €3, €2 under-eights.*

Città della Scienza, via Coroglio 104, **T** 081-3723728, www.cittadellascienza.it *Tue-Sat 0900-1700, Sun 1000-1900, €7.* 12,000 sq m of 'science city' include some excellent hands-on exhibits. Ferrovia Cumana to Bagnoli then bus to Città della Scienza.

Edenlandia, viale Kennedy, **T** 081-2394090, www.edenlandia.it *Jun-Sep, Mon-Fri 1700-0000, Sat-Sun 1030-0000. €4 entrance or €8.30 for tickets including unlimited use of all attractions. Buses C2, C3 and 152 stop outside the park, as does the Ferrovia Cumana (stop "Edenlandia").* Various rides and attractions include a tower, ghost train, castles and 'baby karts'.

Magic World, **T** 081-8047122, www.magicworld.it infomagic@magicworld.it *Jun-Aug Mon-Fri 1000-2200, Sat-Sun 1000-0000. Check website or telephone for opening hours for the rest of the year. €8-€16 depending on age and time.* A theme and aquapark outside the city, *Magic World* is reachable by special bus service from Licola, a station on the Cumana line.

Pompeii, **T** 081-8575347, www.pompeiisites.org, p81. *Apr-Oct 0830-1930, last entrance 1800. Nov-Mar 0830-1700, last entrance 1530. €8.26, including same-day visits to Oplontis, Stabia and Boscoreale.*

Airline offices
Go, **T** 848-887766, www.gofly.com **Ryanair**, www.ryanair.com
Alitalia, **T** 081-7093333/848-865643, www.alitalia.it **British Airways**, **T** 848-812266, www.britishairways.com

Airport information
Aeroporto Internazionale di Napoli, via del Riposo 95,
T 848-888777/081-7515371, **F** 081-7896707, flight information:
T 081-7896259, www.gesac.it customer_service@gesac.it

Banks and ATMs
Almost all cash machines accept all common forms of credit cards.

Bicycle hire
Napoli Bike, riviera di Chiaia 201, **T/F** 081-411934
www.napolibike.com See p205.

Car hire
Avis, Aeroporto di Capodichino **T** 081-7805790; piazza Garibaldi
T 081-5543020. **Hertz**, Aeroporto di Capodichino **T** 081-7802971;
piazza Garibaldi **T** 081-206228. **Maggiore**, Aeroporto di
Capodichino **T** 081-5521900; piazza Garibaldi **T** 081-287858.

Consulates (see also Embassies)
UK, via Francesco Crispi 122, **T** 081-663511. **Canada**, via Carducci
29, **T** 081-401338. **USA**, piazza della Repubblica, **T** 081-5838111.

Credit card lines
There is a single free telephone line for losses of all major types of
credit card: **T** 800207167.

Cultural institutions
British Council, via Crispi 92, **T** 081-667410. **Goethe Institut**,
riviera di Chiaia 202, **T** 081-413943. **Instituto Francese di**

Napoli, via Crispi 86, **T** 081-669665. **Instituto Cervantes**, via San Giacomo 40, **T** 081-5520469.

Disabled

Disabled access in the city is improving but is still generally poor, or poorly thought through. Other destinations around the city fare better, though Roman remains have their own problems. For information about disabled-friendly facilities, transport, hotels and restaurants, the city council's *Passepartout 2000* provides plenty of help and information and the website has some good itineraries. **Galleria Principe di Napoli 33**, **T** 081-5440970, www.pp2000.it   Mon-Fri 0900-1300.

Dentists and doctors

Chemists or hotels should be able to provide you with the name and number of a local English-speaking doctor or dentist.

Electricity

The standard system is 220V, compatible with most UK and US appliances as long as you bring a continental adaptor.

Embassies

Embassies in Rome: Australia **T** 06-852721; Ireland **T** 06-6979121; New Zealand **T** 06-4417171; South Africa **T** 06-852541.

Emergency numbers

Police (Carabinieri), **T** 112. **Fire T** 115. **Ambulance T** 118. **Coast Guard T** 1530.

Hospitals

Both of the following have 24-hour *pronto soccorso* (casualty departments): **Ospedale Cardarelli**, via Antonio Cardarelli 9, **T/F** 081-5464318; **Ospedale Santobono**, via Mario Fiore, **T** 081-2205111.

Internet/email

Mercurio Bookshop, piazzetta Demetrio Salazar 8, **T** 081-2400371, art.slab@tiscalinet.it *Mon 1530-1930; Tue-Sat 1000-1330 and 1530-1930; Sun 1000-1330.* Friendly place just behind piazza del Plebiscito (go up the steps to the left of the Colonnade) has fast internet access for €2 an hour. **Internetbar**, piazza Bellini, **T** 081-295237. *0900-0200 Mon-Sun, www.internetbarnapoli.it €2.50/hr or €20 for 10 hours when you pay in advance.* Has 15 terminals. You have to sign up to become a member, but this is free. It's a proper bar too, so you can sip a beer whilst surfing. **Intra Moenia** (see p155) next door but one. *€2.07/½hr.* Slightly more salubrious surroundings but more expensive. **My Beautiful Laundrette**, via Montesanto 2, **T** 081-5422162, mybeautifullaundrette@yahoo.it *€3.10 per wash/dry, internet €2.50/hr.* For a more unusual internet experience – access while you do your washing.

Language schools

Centro di lingua e cultura italiana, vico Santa Maria dell'Aiuto 17, **T** 081-5524331. They offer good selection of both long and short courses.

Left luggage

Stazione Centrale, **T** 081-5672181. Open 24hrs a day.

Libraries

Biblioteca Nazionale in the Palazzo Reale, **T** 081-401273. *Mon-Fri 0830-1930, Sat 0830-1330. Photo ID required for entry.* An exceptionally grand old library, holding 2,000 papyri from Herculaneum and parts of a Bible in 5th-century Coptic.

Lost property

For anything lost on a train there is an office at the Stazione Centrale, **T** 081-5672366. For anything left on a bus, tram or metro in the city, call **T** 800639525/081-7632177. For anything else go to the nearest police station.

Motorcycle hire
Renting scooters in Naples is almost impossible due to the threat of theft. On the islands, the Amalfi Coast and in Sorrento there are lots of companies who usually rent by the day.

Media
Il Mattino, www.ilmattino.it   Neapolitan-based daily with a good listings section. **English language newspapers** are available from some newsstands, particularly on via Toledo and in piazza dei Martiri and all over Sorrento, the Amalfi Coast and the islands, though they are usually European editions, and always a day behind. Free dailies **Leggo** and **City** are also available (especially at stations) and have a reasonable amount of national and inter-national news, though less about Naples itself. They're good if you want to check the weather forecast or football scores though. A handful of local TV stations pump out absolute pap.

Pharmacies (late-night)
Identified by a large green cross outside. There is a rotation of pharmacies which are open outside normal hours. **T** 1100 for addresses of three nearest open pharmacies. There are also lists in *Il Mattino* and on the doors of pharmacies. *Normal hours are Mon-Fri 0830-1300, 1600-2000, Sat 0830-1300.*

Police
You can always speak to an operator in English on the emergency number **T** 112. The **Questura Centrale** (central police station) is at via Medina 75, **T** 081-7941111.

Post offices
The central post office is the big fascist-era building on piazza

Matteotti. *Mon-Sat 0815-1920*. There is also a post office in the Galleria Umberto. Expect long queues. Stamps are also available from tabacchi.

Public holidays

In August, as in much of the rest of Italy, Naples abandons the city and heads for the seaside. Many shops will be closed for some or all of the month, as are restaurants and many clubs and bars move to the beach.

Most shops and museums etc will be closed on the days listed below. Transport may run on a Sunday timetable, but don't rely on this. 1 January: Capodanno, New Year's Day. 6 January, Befana, Epiphany. Easter: Pasquetta, Easter Monday. 25 April: Festa della Liberazione, Liberation Day. 1 May: Festa del Lavoro, Labour Day. 15 August: Ferragosto, Feast of the Assumption. 19 September: Festa di San Gennaro, Feast Day of St Gennaro, Naples' patron saint. 1 November: Ognissanti, All Saints Day. 8 December: L'Immacolata, Feast of the Immaculate Conception. 25 December: Natale, Christmas Day. 26 December: Santo Stefano, Boxing Day.

Religious services

Most Neapolitan churches post the times of their services outside the door. Mass is held in English in the St Francis De Geronimo Hall, near Chiesa Gesù Nuovo, every Sunday and feast day at 1645.

Student organizations

Centro Turistico Studentesco giovanile (CTS), via Mezzocannone 25, **T** 081-5527960. Mainly a travel agency, but will also give information and general help.

Telephone

In Italy it's now necessary to use area codes no matter where you phone from. Hence you need to dial the code for Naples (081) even from within the city. Numbers in this book are given with the code. To call Italy from abroad you no longer drop the initial '0' of the code as you do for other countries. To call home from Italy dial 00 plus the country code (UK 44, Australia 61, Canada/ USA 1, Irish Republic 353) before dialling the number. The **Europa** phone card is excellent value for phoning home. Available from tabacchi (ask for "*una scheda col codice Europa*") it gives you 3 hours of calls anywhere in Europe or America for just €5. Careful using it with mobiles though – your phone company may charge you for the usually freephone 800 number it uses. Most public phones use **Telecom Italia** cards rather than coins. The cheapest card is €5. Mobiles with international romaing activated will work but prices are high both to make and receive calls.

Time

Italy uses **Central European Time**, one hour ahead of Greenwich Mean Time. Daylight saving comes into operation in the summer in synch with the rest of Europe.

Tipping

Only the more expensive restaurants will necessarily expect a tip though everywhere will be grateful for one. Ten to fifteen per cent is the norm. A few spare coins when ordering a coffee might speed the process up. Taxis may add on extra costs for you anyway but a little extra is always appreciated. Rounding prices up always goes down well, especially if it means avoiding having to give change, not a favourite Italian habit.

Toilets

Public toilets are few and far between, free ones even more so. Make use of those in cafés, bars, restaurants, museums and stations. In the centre of Naples the Palazzo Reale has good, clean and free toilets.

Transport enquiries
General train information: **T** 848888088 (0700-2100 daily).
Club Eurostar: **T** 081-286996. **Circumvesuviana**:
T 081-7722444. **Ferrovia Cumana/Circumflegrea**:
T 800001616. **Metronapoli/Funicolari**: **T** 800568866. **SITA buses**: **T** 081-5522176. **City (CTP) buses**: **T** 081-7001111. **ANM buses**: **T** 081-7631111. **Radiotaxi**: **T** 081-5525252.

Travel agents
Most travel agents in Naples will have at least one person who speaks some English. Outside the city they are likely to be fluent. **CTS**, via Mezzocannone 25, **T** 081-5527960. Specializes in student and young-person travel and is a good place to start looking for discount tickets and travel information.

A sprint through history

8th century BC	Greeks colonize Ischia, calling it Pithekoussai. Subsequently they found mainland Cumae and Parthenope near modern Pizzofalcone in Naples.
524 BC and 474 BC	Battles between the Etruscans and the Greeks are fought at Cumae, both won by the Greeks.
c470 BC	The Greeks found Neapolis ("New City"), whose original street-plan can still be seen in the Centro Storico of contemporary Naples.
328BC	The Romans lay siege to Neapolis, which falls two years later.
312BC	Construction of the Appian Way is begun, linking Rome to the south, and to fashionable Hellenic-style education and holidays.
89-82BC	Neapolis and other Campanian towns take sides against Rome and are brutally occupied by Sulla, leader of the Roman army.
AD 27-37	Emperor Tiberius builds a villa on Capri and decides to stay, moving the seat of power to the island.
AD 79	Vesuvius erupts, burying Pompeii and other nearby towns in lava, dust, mud and ash.
5th century	Goths take sporadic control of Neapolis. Vandal attackers lay waste to Capua in 456. The last Roman Emperor, Romulus Augustus, imprisoned by Goth King, Odoacer, dies in Naples in 476.
AD 536	Naples falls to Byzantine Emperor Justinian.
AD 581, 592 and 599	Lombards from north of the Alps lay siege unsuccessfully to Naples. Naples also comes under attack from north African Saracens.

645	Basilio becomes the first native Duke of Neapolis, by the power of the Byzantine Emperor. Naples is more self-determining, and flourishes.
8th–10th centuries	The city is largely successful in playing its various enemies off against each other, while growing in wealth itself.
10th century	Amalfi becomes an increasingly independent entity, allied to Byzantium, but with an ever-growing naval presence.
1062	The Normans, now without support from Naples, take Capua, followed in 1073 by Amalfi and in 1077 by Salerno.
1130	A Norman is crowned King Roger II of Sicily.
1139	Neapolitans swear allegiance to the Sicillian crown, which now controls most of southern Italy. Much of Naples' power slips south to Palermo.
1194	Tancred, last of the Normans, dies. Henry of Swabia, son of the Holy Roman Emperor, takes control.
1214	Frederick II, son of Henry of Swabia, takes on joint mantel of Holy Roman Emperor and King of Southern Italy. He invests in Naples, establishing a new university.
1251	Naples declares itself a free commune rather than accepting German rule of Frederick's son Conrad. Two years later, Imperial forces win Naples back.
1256	Charles of Anjou takes control of Sicily, and Naples pledges itself to the new French power in the region. Charles moves the capital from Palermo back to Naples and invests in the city, building the Castel Nuovo.

1302	Charles gives up control of Sicily to the Aragonese.
1442	Alfonso of Aragon, King of Sicily, takes control of Naples, unifying southern Italy once again.
1494	Naples' nobles, opposing Spanish control, persuade France's King Charles VIII to occupy the city, but the Neapolitan people rebel against this new authority and reinstall an Aragonese king, Ferdinand II.
1501	When, after Ferdinand's death, Naples' nobles give the crown to his uncle Frederick, the Spanish march on the city and King Ferdinand of Spain becomes King Ferdinand III of Naples.
1502	Ferdinand III leaves a viceroy in Naples. Spanish viceroys come to be hated over the next 250 years.
1600	Naples, with a population of over 300,000, becomes Europe's biggest city.
1631	Vesuvius erupts, killing around 3,500 people.
1647	Masaniello, a stall-holder, sparks a revolt in the city by declaring one of Spain's many taxes void. He is assassinated nine days later but revolts continue all over southern Italy.
1656	Plague kills three-quarters of the population.
1707	Austria occupies Naples, imposing more viceroys.
1734	Teenage Charles Bourbon, son of Philip V of Spain, expels Austrians and becomes Charles III of the Kingdom of Sicily, with Naples as its capital.
1737	Charles builds the San Carlo opera house.
1748	Systematic excavation of Pompeii is started, following amazing finds at Herculaneum.
1757	Charles abdicates to succeed his father in Spain.

1768	Maria Carolina, daughter of the Austrian empress, arrives in Naples to marry Charles' son Ferdinand.
1793	Maria Carolina's sister, Marie Antoinette, is executed in Paris, and Naples joins the anti-French alliance.
1798	A Neapolitan army takes Rome from the French, but only for 11 days.
1799	The French enter the city and the liberal Repubblica Partenopea is declared. The royal family escape to Sicily aboard Nelson's ship. After the republicans agree to a capitulation, over 200 are executed by Nelson and the returning royal family.
1806	The French, under Joseph Bonaparte, occupy Naples. The royals escape to Sicily again.
1816	Following the council of Vienna, Ferdinand returns, under the new title of King Ferdinand I of the Kingdom of the Two Sicilies.
1848	Naples' parliament demands a constitution and a year later Ferdinand's son, Ferdinand II, dissolves it.
1859	Ferdinand II's son Francesco comes to the throne.
1860	On 7 September, Garibaldi and the unification troops enter the city to an enthusiastic welcome. Just over a month later, Naples votes in favour of joining a united Italy.
1884	Naples suffers a serious cholera outbreak.
1880-1914	Italian emigration to America totals around two and a half million, many from the south.
1943	Allied bombs devastate the city. In the *Quattro giornate napoletane*, Naples' citizens liberate their own city from the Germans.

1943-49	As many as a third of Naples' women are forced into prostitution to survive. In the liberated power vacuum, the black market and the Camorra flourish.
1944	Vesuvius erupts, killing 26 people.
1946	In a referendum 80% of Neapolitans vote to keep the monarchy, but nationally the vote is lost and Vittorio Emanuele, the son of King Umberto II, Italy's last king, sails from Naples to join his father in exile.
1950s-93	With few interruptions, a Christian Democrat/Camorra alliance controls the city. Large amounts of development and industrialization take place, mostly without regulation or planning permission.
1973	Another cholera epidemic hits the city.
1980	An earthquake kills 3,000 and leaves thousands homeless for months.
1992	The *Mani Pulite* (Clean Hands) enquiries into corruption begin around Italy.
1993	Left-winger Antonio Bassolino is elected mayor, and sparks the so-called Neapolitan Renaissance.
1994	The G7 Summit is held in Naples and creates impetus for Bassolino's reforms.
2001	'No Global' protests at the Global Forum being held in the city turn into riots and over a hundred people are injured.
2002	Eight police are arrested for their part in the alleged torture of 'No Global' protesters, who were allegedly dragged out of hospital following the March 2001 riots.

Art and architecture

8th century BC	Greeks and Etruscans both arrive in the south of Italy. At Cuma, in the Campi Flegrei, the Greeks build temples on a hill around the cave of their Sibyl. Ruins of the temples can still be seen along with the remarkable cave.
6th century BC	South of Naples, Paestum is founded. Temples and frescoes from the Tomb of the Diver still survive. Paestum's Doric style is later influential on neoclassical architecture.
c470BC	Neapolis (later to become Naples) is founded. The Greek agora (marketplace) was approximately where piazza San Gaetano stands today. Remains of Greek walls can be seen in piazza Bellini, and parts of the Greek city are visible below Roman remains in the Scavi di San Lorenzo Maggiore.
100BC–100 AD	Campania becomes the playground of Rome and many villas and palaces are built in the area.
79AD	Eruption of Vesuvius buries Pompeii, Herculaneum, Oplontis and Stabia, preserving them and countless mosaics, statues and frescoes. Some of the finest surviving examples of Roman art are also preserved just outside Pompeii at the Villa dei Misteri.
2nd century	Paintings in the catacombs of San Gennaro date from a time when Christianity was literally an underground movement.
4th century	The spread of Christianity means the construction of more religious buildings. Churches change from ancient temples by moving the columns inside.

1279	As Naples becomes capital of the Anjou kingdom (1256), construction of the Castel Nuovo is started. More great buildings rise over the next hundred years, including the Duomo, many churches, and the Castel Sant'Elmo. Many artists are brought in from France and northern Italy.
13th century	To the south, Amalfi and Ravello become rich, fed by trade and naval might, and many villas and churches are built. Moorish influences can still be seen, for example in Ravello's Villa Rufolo.
1328-34	Giotto works in the city as court painter. Little of his work survives, though his influence continues to be felt after his departure.
1450	Alfonso of Aragon, a humanist, becomes king and brings with him Renaissance ideas. The Renaissance leaves behind some fine work in Naples (still to be seen, especially in the Museo di Capodimonte, the triumphal arch of Castel Nuovo and the church of Sant'Anna dei Lombardi) but it essentially remains a Tuscan movement, never really becoming ingrained in Neapolitan culture.
1606	Caravaggio flees Rome where he is wanted for murder and comes to Naples. Though he stays less than a year his influence is enormous. His simmering study of brutality, *Flagellation* (Capodimonte), and *The Seven Acts of Mercy* (Pio Monte della Misericordia) are two of Naples' most important paintings.
17th century	A close group of Neapolitan painters led by Jusepe de Ribera, Belisario Corenzio and Battistello Caracciolo, and clearly influenced by Caravaggio, become important figures in the city's art.

1630	Artemisia Gentileschi, one of the very few successful female painters of the time, comes to Naples where she lives until her death in 1653. Her dramatic and influential *Judith and Holofernes* is in the Museo di Capodimonte.
1656	In the aftermath of devastating plague, Naples' desire to rebuild and to celebrate the ornate and the extravagant, rather than the life-like and the natural, gives strength to its acceptance of the Baroque. This period is probably Naples' most successful in artistic and architectural terms – it is a movement that fits the dramatic psyche of the city perhaps better than any other.
1660	Cosimo Fanzago's Baroque and very Neapolitan Guglia di San Gennaro is erected in piazza Riario Sforza. It is one of three of these strange spires around the centre of Naples. Fanzago, Naples' foremost Baroque architect, spends much of his career on the Certosa di San Martino.
Late 16th-17th century	The church and chapels in the Certosa di San Martino are decorated by the best Neapolitan artists of the time. They remain showpieces of the height of Neapolitan Baroque.
1737	The Teatro di San Carlo is built by Charles III. He also commissions palaces at Caserta and Capodimonte as well as the Albergo dei Poveri which, even though only a fifth of it is ever built, is the largest building in southern Europe.
18th century	Landscape painting, particularly scenes of the Bay of Naples, Vesuvius, or of Naples from the sea, becomes very fashionable.

18th-19th century	The Grand Tour, an artistic and historic visit to Italy, becomes a vital part of a young English gentleman's education. Artists also come from the north to see the sights and the scenery, among them Turner, who stays in Naples for a month.
1890	The Galleria Umberto, a massive four-armed glass and iron domed arcade, is built opposite the Teatro di San Carlo, partly to resurrect an area devastated by a cholera epidemic in 1884.
1942-43	Allied bombing destroys many monuments in the Centro Storico.
1950s	The *Hotel Jolly* is built, central Naples' most conspicuous eyesore. This building is given planning permission but in many other cases buildings are put up illegally and a post-war concrete jungle spreads around the bay.
1960s	Andy Warhol paints a pop-art version of Vesuvius erupting (Capodimonte).
1980s	The Centro Direzionale is conceived as a shiny new business centre (designed by Japanese architect Kenzo Tange) to the north of the station. It is much criticized and remains soulless and incomplete.
1993	Reforming mayor Bassolino is elected into office and invests in contemporary work, including Jannis Kounelli's windmill in largo Ponte di Tappia. He also encourages the opening of many of the city's monuments, churches and other buildings, closed to the public for years.

Books

Acton, H, *The Bourbons of Naples* (Methuen, 1956; Prion, 1998) A slightly lengthy but well-documented historical account of the rulers of Napoleon-era Naples.

Boccaccio, G, *The Decameron* (1350; Penguin, 1995 eds. McWilliam, G H and George Henry) Boccaccio's 14th-century collection of bawdy stories is one of the classics of Italian literature, a kind of Mediterranean Arabian Nights, and some of the best stories are set in Naples.

Burns, J, *Hand of God: the Life of Maradona* (Bloomsbury, 1996) A cut above the average sports biography, this is an insightful look at the Maradona phenomenon, dealing with everything from his Camorra connections to his sublime ball skills.

Casanova, G, *History of My Life Vols I and II* In this memoir, Casanova tells tales of his youth in Padua, Venice, Corfu, and Milan as well as Naples. It is an account of political intrigue, literature, art, philosophy, and, of course, love, but also how to make good hot chocolate. ISBN 0801856620

Corrivetti, C, *Occhi su Napoli/Focus on Naples* A beautifully produced photographic book on Naples, documenting the art, the monuments, the streets and the people of the city in both colour and black and white. It has occasional quotes about the city in Italian and English, and even comes in a slipcase. May be hard to find abroad. ISBN 8886795084

Croce, B, *Estetica* (Cambridge UP, 1992) One of the most important works in the philosophical study of aesthetics, this book by Naples' greatest philosopher is also a general theory of everything: the intrinsic connection between the mind, society and art.

Hazzard, S, *Greene on Capri* (Virago, 2000) The relationship between Graham Greene, the island of Capri, and his writing is explored in this intelligent book written by a friend he met there.

Lewis, N, *Naples '44* (William Collins, 1978; Eland, 2002) The renowned travel writer writes here about his time in Naples after the liberation of 1944. The way the Allied forces turned a blind eye to, or even encouraged, the Camorra in order to try to maintain order explains a lot about the modern city.

Munthe, A, *The Story of San Michele* (John Murray, 1929) This foreigner-living-abroad tale, first published in 1929, still has thousands of loyal fans, many of whom visit the Villa of San Michele on Capri (see p101), to see it for themselves. Thousands more, never having heard of the book, visit the villa anyway and then buy the book on their return home. All in all it's the centre of a thriving industry.

Sontag, S, *Volcano Lover* (Jonathan Cape, 1992) Based on the famous love triangle of Sir William Hamilton, his wife, Emma, and Lord Nelson, this is a historical romance, but also covers opera, Goethe and, of course, volcanoes.

Tippett, J, *Sorrento and the Amalfi Coast: Walks, Tours and Picnics* (Sunflower, 1996) Despite an occasionally twee feel, this is an excellent and easy-to-use guide to the numerous good walking possibilities on the Sorrento Peninsula, the Amalfi Coast and Capri. Good maps are included.

Vico, G, *New Science* (Cornell UP, 1948, trans. from the 3rd ed. (1744)) This humanist philosophical work by one of Naples' greatest philosophers inspired James Joyce's *Finnegan's Wake*. It deals with the development of cultures, societies and language, and is now seen increasingly as one of Italy's most important philosophical works.

Language

In hotels and bigger restaurants, you'll usually find English is spoken. In Naples you may not find it spoken elsewhere that much but on the islands, in Sorrento and on the Amalfi Coast, you shouldn't have too many problems.

But Naples also has its own language – **Neapolitan**. Really it's a dialect, but you can buy Italian-Neapolitan dictionaries in the bookshops, and it's certainly different enough that even with good Italian you will sometimes find yourself surrounded by a strange clipped tongue which you can't follow at all. Influenced by Spanish, French and even Arabic it's one of the most widely spoken of the Italian dialects.

Basics

thank you *grazie*
hi/goodbye *ciao*
good day (until after lunch/mid-afternoon) *buongiorno*
good evening (after lunch) *buonasera*
goodnight *buonanotte*
goodbye *arrivederci*
please *per favore*
I'm sorry *mi dispiace*
excuse me *permesso*
yes *si*
no *no*

Numbers

one *uno*, two *due*, three *tre*, four *quattro*, five *cinque*, six *sei*, seven *sette*, eight *otto*, nine *nove*, 10 *dieci*, 11 *undici*, 12 *dodici*, 13 *tredici*, 14 *quattordici*, 15 *quindici*, 16 *sedici*, 17 *diciassette*, 18 *diciotto*, 19 *diciannove*, 20 *venti*, 21 *ventuno*, 22 *ventidue*, 30 *trenta*, 40 *quaranta*, 50 *cinquanta*, 60 *sessanta*, 70 *settanta*, 80 *ottanta*, 90 *novanta*, 100 *cento*, 200 *due cento*, 1000 *mille*.

Questions

how? *come?*
how much? *quanto?*
when? *quando?*
where? *dove?*
why? *perché?*
what? *Che cosa?*

Problems

I don't understand *Non capisco*
I don't know *Non lo so*
I don't speak Italian *Non parlo italiano*
How do you say …(in Italian)? *Come si dice … (in italiano)?*
Is there anyone who speaks English? *C'è qualcuno che parla inglese?*

Shopping

this one/that one *questo/quello*
less *meno*
more *di più*
How much is it/are they? *quanto costa/costano?*
Can I have …? *posso avere …?*

Eating/drinking

Can I have the bill? *posso avere il conto?*
What's this? *cos'è questo?*
Is there a menu? *c'è un menù?*
Where's the toilet? *dov'è il bagno?*

Hotels

a double/single room *una camera doppia/singola*
a double bed *un letto matrimoniale*
bathroom *bagno*
Is there a view? *c'è una bella vista?*

Can I see the room? *posso vedere la camera?*
When is breakfast? *a che ora è la colazione?*
Can I have the key? *posso avere la chiave?*

Time
morning *mattina*
afternoon *pommeriggio*
evening *sera*
night *notte*
soon *presto/fra poco*
later *più tardi*
What time is it? *Che ore sono?*
today/tomorrow/yesterday *oggi/domani/ieri*

Gestures
Italians are famously theatrical and animated in dialogue and often resort to a variety of gestures in order to accompany or in some cases substitute words. Knowing a few of these will help you both to understand what's being implied to you and also to become more Italian during your stay.

Side of left palm on side of right wrist as right wrist is flicked up
Go away
Hunched shoulders and arms lifted with palms of hands outwards What am I supposed to do?
Thumb, index and middle finger of hand together, wrist upturned and shaking What the hell are you doing/what's going on?
Both palms together and moved up and down in front of stomach Ditto
All fingers of hand squeezed together To signify a place is packed full of people
Front of side of hand to chin To signify 'nothing', as in 'I don't understand' or 'I've had enough'
Flicking back of right ear To signify someone is gay
Index finger in cheek To signify good food

Index

Bold page number denotes main entry

Credits

Footprint credits

Text editor: Sarah Thorowgood
Series editor: Rachel Fielding

Production: Jo Morgan, Mark Thomas
In-house cartography: Claire Benison,
Kevin Feeney, Robert Lunn,
Sarah Sorensen
Proof-reading: Judith Wardman

Design: Mytton Williams
Maps: adapted from original cartography
by Netmaps SA, Barcelona, Spain

Photography credits

Front cover: Lonely Planet Images
Inside: Julius Honnor
Generic images: John Matchett
Back cover: Julius Honnor (Vesuvius from
Santa Lucia)

Print

Manufactured in Italy by Rotolito
Lombarda, Italy

Publishing information

Footprint Naples
1st edition
Text and maps © Footprint Handbooks
Ltd November 2002

ISBN 1 903471 46 X
CIP DATA: a catalogue record for this
book is available from the British Library

Published by Footprint Handbooks
6 Riverside Court
Lower Bristol Road
Bath, BA2 3DZ, UK
T +44 (0)1225 469141
F +44 (0)1225 469461
E discover@footprintbooks.com
W www.footprintbooks.com

Distributed in the USA by
Publishers Group West

Publishing stuff

For a different view…
choose a Footprint

Over 80 Footprint travel guides
Covering more than 145 of the world's most exciting
countries and cities in Latin America, the Caribbean, Africa, Indian
sub-continent, Australasia, North America, Southeast Asia, the
Middle East and Europe.

Discover so much more…
The finest writers. In-depth knowledge. Entertaining and accessible.
Critical restaurant and hotels reviews. Lively descriptions of all the
attractions. Get away from the crowds.

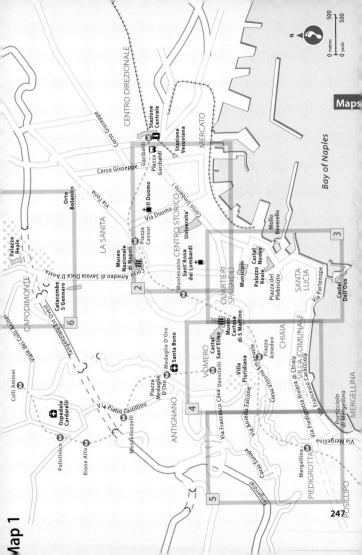

Map 1

Maps

N

500 metres
500 yards

Bay of Naples

247

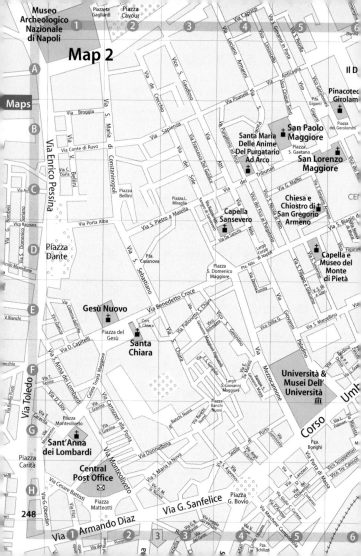

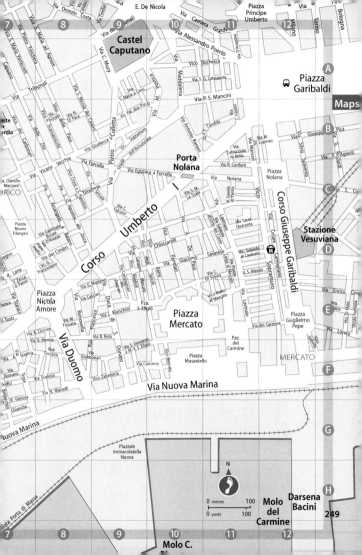

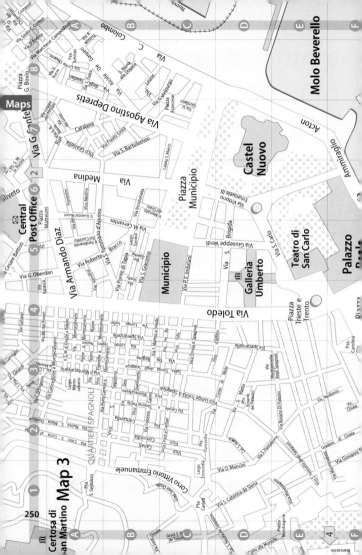

Certosa di
San Martino **Map 3**

Molo Beverello

Castel
Nuovo

Piazza
Municipio

Municipio

Galleria
Umberto

Teatro di
San Carlo

Palazzo
Reale

Piazza
Trieste e
Trento

Via Toledo

QUARTIERI SPAGNOLI

Corso Vittorio Emanuele

Central
Post Office

Via Armando Diaz

Via Agostino Depretis

Piazza
G. Bovio

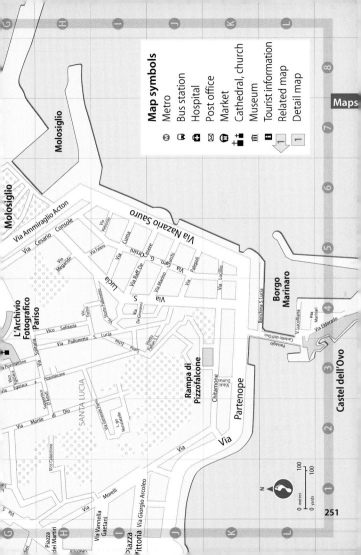

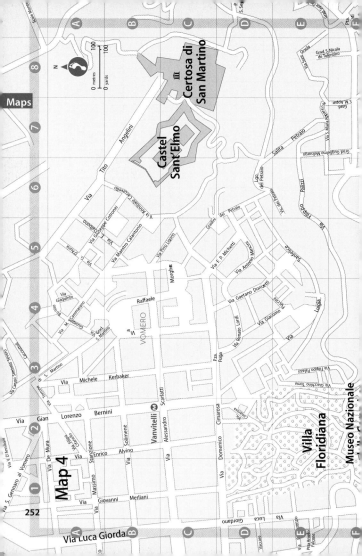

Map 4

252

Certosa di
San Martino

Castel
Sant'Elmo

VOMERO

Villa
Floridiana

Museo Nazionale

N

0 metres   100
0 yards   100

Via S. Gennaro al Vomero
Via V. D'Annibale
Via De-Mura
Via Carlo Cima
Gian Lorenzo Bernini
Vanvitelli
Alessandro Scarlatti
Via Enrico Alvino
Via Solimene
Via Domenico Cimarosa
Via Stanzione
Via Massimo Stanzione
Via Giovanni Merliani
Via Luca Giordano
Via Luca Giordano
Vaccaro

Via Cesare Antonio Serrao
Ceccano
Via di S. Giuseppe
Via di S. Martino
Via Michele Kerbaker
Via M. Schipa
Via M. Schipa
Via Giacinto Gigante
Via F. D'Andrea
Raffaele
Morghen
Via Fermo Lacrio
Via Giuseppe Cotronei
Via Maestro Galantomo
Via Antonio Maiuri
Via F. P. Michetti
Via Antonio Manci
Via Gaetano Donizetti
Via Renato Lordi
Via Giacomo
Luigia
Via
Via
Via Giacinto Toma
Via Filippo Palazzi
Pza. Fuga
Gradini del Petraio
Salita Petraio
Grad. del Petraio
Tirsa del Petraio
Sanfelice
Via Filippo Palizzi
Grad. Guglielmo Melisurgo
Via S. Maria Apparente
Grad. S. M. Appar.
Via San Carlo
Grad. S. Nicola de Tolentino
Orsola
Pza. Tr
Angelini
Tito
Via
Salita Moiariello

A B C D E F

1 2 3 4 5 6 7 8

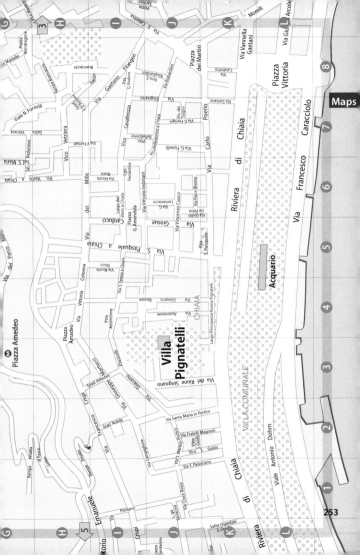

Map 5

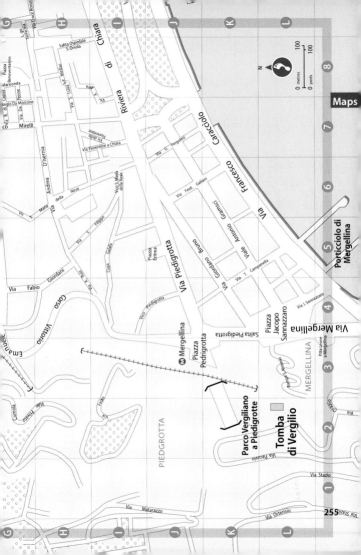

G H I J K L

8

7

6

5

4

3

2

1

N
0 metres 100
0 yards 100

Porticciolo di Mergellina

Via Croce Rossa
Salita Ospedale
S. Orsola
Riviera di Chiara
Via Luigi S. Mutillo
Via Fra
Piazza
Beneventano
Pgo B. di Lgo Da Morcone
Via Da Morcone
Co Mirelli
Andrea D'Isernia
Via Maria della Neve
Via S. Maria della Neve
Via Filippo
Via Delle Fiorentine
Via Fiorentine a Chiaia
Vlc
Giordani
Corso Vittorio
Via Fabio
Emanuele
Carmela
Viale Trinità
Via T. Tasso
Cupa
Galfà
Piazza Eritrea
Via Piedigrotta
Via Giordano Bruno
Via Antonio Gramsci
Viale
Via J. Sannazzaro
Via Ferd. Galiani
Via G. Pergolesi
Via Caracciolo Francesco
Via Campanella
Piazza Jacopo Sannazzaro
Via Mergellina
MERGELLINA
Pta Leone a Mergellina
Rampe S. Antonio
Via Orazio
M Mergellina
Piazza Pedigrotta
Salita Piedigrotta
Vico Piedigrotta
Via Erbo
PIEDGROTTA
Via Matarazzo
Via Paturio
Via Stazio
Via Ortensio
Via Stazio

Parco Vergiliano a Piedigrotte

Tomba di Vergilio

255

Map 6

Via Gaetano Manfredi
Via Pio XXII
Via Gennaro Marciano
Viale del Colli Aminei
Via F. Curia
Via del Colli Aminei
Parco di Capodimonte
Via di Miano
Palazzo Reale
Via S. Antonio a Capodimonte
Salita di Capodimonte
Via di Capodimonte
Tondo di Capodimonte
Parco Jolanda Gradini
Piazzale Capodimonte Madre Landi
Corso Amedeo di Savoia Duca D'Aosta
Via Vincenzo Gemito
Vico dei Pizzocoli
Piazza S. Severo a Capodimonte
Vicolo Tronari

Catacombe S. Gennaro
Vicolo S. Gennaro dei Poveri
S. Gennaro dei Poveri
Via Di Mauro

Viale Letizia
Quercet.
P. le

Via Ignazio
Via L. A. Astore
Via Gen.
Via C. Cimino
Via di Caballi
Via A. Genovesi
Via Nicola Nicolini
Via Carlo De Marco
Via Ponti Rossi
V.le Traetta
Via Ponti Rossi
Via F. Traetta
Cupa Macedonia
Via Ponti Rossi
Cupa Eterno Padre

Piazza Ottocalli
Via Arenaccia
Piazza S. Giovanni e Paolo
Falconieri
Via Abate Minchini
Piazza Romo
Via Scipione Volpicella
Via Giacomo Gravina
Via Giambattista Vico
Piazza Macedonia
Via Severino Marco Aurelio
Via S. Eframo Vecchio
Via Pier delle Vigne
Via Bernardo Tanucci
Vico S. Eframo Vecchio
Vico Nettuno
Vico Zurlo
Cupa Michele Guardato
Cupa S. Eframo Vecchio
Vico S. Eframo Vecchio
Piazza S. Eframo Vecchio
Strada Veterinaria
Via Fabio Galeota
Via Paradisiello
Via Montagna

Via Tenz.
Via Zita
Via G. Travaglini Forgès
Via Don Bosco
Via Giovanni Giusmo
Via G. Gen.
Via Ma.
Via Alex
Via Arenaccia
Via Gaetano Argento
Piazza Carlo III
Corso Giuseppe
Attanasio
Via S. Alfonso Maria De' Liguori
Pza Maria De' Liguori
Giannone
Via Fe.
Andre
Via G. Silvati
Orto Botanico
Via Michele Te.
Via Salita Fo.
Pino
Via O. Morisani
Rampe Oliero Morisani
Salita Miradois
Vico Salita Miradois
Salita de la Ficora

N